THE
PSYCHOLOGICAL
ASPECTS OF ABORTION

THE PSYCHOLOGICAL ASPECTS OF ABORTION

Editors:
David Mall
Walter F. Watts, M.D.

Sponsored by
Department of Obstetrics and Gynecology
Stritch School of Medicine
Loyola University

UNIVERSITY PUBLICATIONS OF AMERICA, INC.

ISBN: 0-89093-298-0

Library of Congress Catalog Card Number: 79-88679

Manufactured in the United States of America

Contents

Preface

On October 31, 1978, ten American and Canadian specialists in psychiatry and related disciplines assembled in Chicago at the invitation of the Stritch School of Medicine of Loyola University. For two days they presented papers and exchanged views in a symposium on the psychological aspects of abortion.

In developing the symposium agenda, the editors were pleased with the interest shown by all who were originally invited and, of course, were doubly pleased with those who actually found time in their busy schedules to participate. All who could not come wished us well and regretted prior commitments.

The purpose of the symposium was underlined at a press conference attended by the participants early in the first day's program. When asked about the presence of any major post-abortion studies concerning psychiatric sequelae, the consensus was that no comprehensive data existed. It was the absence of such data that gave the symposium its chief justification. Accordingly, because the medical community has been slow in addressing this scarcity of information, what is contained herein is an attempt to help correct a serious deficiency in the literature.

While sensitive to the need for scientific detachment in the reporting of undesirable sequelae, the editors are fully aware of the controversial nature of the topic. By good fortune, they were able to assemble participants who happened to be members of the three major faiths found in North America—Protestant, Catholic, Jew—to help dispel any charge of religious bias. This variety of religious experience attests to the fact that, although what emerged from the symposium was highly critical of elective abortion as performed in American today, the results were certainly not programmatically Catholic, or even Christian.

While the papers touch upon the major themes of the discussion as they have emerged over the years, one editor felt at liberty to add some thoughts of his own. The thoughts contained in this essay are insights from a non-medical perspective. They are part of the penumbra of the discussion and will aid the reader's understanding. The essay is intended to be supplementary.

The editors wish to thank all those who helped make the symposium and its literary outcome a success, especially Phyllis Taylor and Violet Ozgowicz, who interrupted their office routines to handle problems needing immediate attention, and Margaret Klein and Michael Budde, who helped with the manuscript.

A special thanks is extended to Sandra Mahkorn for accommodating her busy academic schedule to meeting the publisher's deadline. Her essay on rape was commissioned too late to be read at the symposium, but was enthusiastically received by the editors in time to be included here.

If this book stimulates further critical thinking and dispels some of the myths surrounding the psychological aspects of abortion, it will have achieved its objective and rendered society an important service by adding a carefully modulated scientific voice to the growing national debate.

Introduction

Ralph Waldo Emerson maintained that the world belongs to those who see through its pretense. In 1973 this observation was put to the test by the U.S. Supreme Court in *Roe* v. *Wade*. Since that time the chief reason given for most abortions obtained in America is the highly indeterminate category of psychological need.

With this book, the reader will confront for the first time an important accumulation of new scientific evidence pointing to a rethinking of America's policy regarding abortion. The essays which follow challenge the conventional wisdom that abortion is psychologically safe. It is not, the writers contend, as simple as having a tooth pulled or one's tonsils removed. Such disarming analogies trivialize the abortion procedure and run counter to years of clinical experience.

The writers claim from different perspectives that the case for abortion has not been proved and that what is touted as a safe and simple procedure actually produces its own psychic morbidity. They have searched the psychiatric literature in vain to find one bona fide psychiatric condition for which abortion is a recognized cure. They present some disturbing facts which cry out for attention.

Like a brain scanner projecting variable angles of vision, the levels of analysis provided by each essay help build a profile of the psychological impact of abortion. In analyses both divergent and complementary, the picture of abortion in all its subtlety is brought into increasingly sharper focus. What the reader will see is profound and chilling. And if the book points to anything at all, it is the sad fact that medicine is being manipulated by society. The decision-making apparatus of government has unwittingly rushed to judgment on the abortion question and more data is urgently needed.

Negative data, which this book represents, is vital to the growth of a healthy science, is just as important as positive findings, and should be sought with enthusiasm. Unfortunately, there has been little or no contrary opinion in the abortion debate. What is most disturbing to the writers, however, is that science has chosen to view normal pregnancy as a pathological condition. Any science which does this has lost a vital hold on reality and has become insensitive to sound scientific reasoning. If seriously entertained, such distorted thinking has a tendency to pervade other areas of medicine. Rarely does it occur in isolation.

Paradigmatic of the abortion phenomenon and one used frequently by the advocates of abortion are the problems of rape and incest. The abortion counselor finds these affronts to normal sexual functioning and human dignity the kind of grotesque abnormalities which seem to make abortion immensely worthwhile from a simple humanitarian viewpoint. Lost in the outpouring of propaganda is the wisdom that difficult cases make bad law—a truth not lost sight of by the British House of Commons, which refused to legislate in this area.

A genuine contribution to the growing literature on rape is the study by Mahkorn. Her findings present a stark contrast to the fear and gloom often associated with the problem of sexual assault. In a candid analysis from actual cases, she shows that pregnancy from rape need not devastate the victim and that abortion could, in fact, even compound feelings of guilt and self-blame. Her message is clear and encouraging: The extremely rare instance of rape pregnancy can be dealt with successfully.

In another essay possessed of both depth and scope, Maloof analyses the dark and debilitating narcissism of incest. From his experience as a family counselor, he argues persuasively that incest can best be understood in light of the nature of the family, which, when functioning properly, should provide an environment for the healthy development of the human personality. A family turned inward through incest impairs the contribution each member owes to the whole and to the building of an integrated society. The answer, he writes, lies not in aborting a rare incestuous pregnancy but in helping the incestuous family to grow outward.

The most serious indictment of the current literature, particularly those studies which justify abortion, is the heavy reliance upon the survey method. Neisser and Sim in one essay, and Fisher in another, criticize this reliance methodologically and from their own continuing depth studies. These writers contend that the current psychological follow-ups of women who have had abortions are superficial and unreliable indicators of proper therapy.

Arguments based on survey data have a hollow ring when confronted by the facts of prognosis. It can be easily demonstrated that postpartum patients do better than post-abortion patients in psychotherapy. Abortion puts women at greater risk mentally, and to conclude otherwise is to go beyond available data.*

If the mark of a good book on abortion is how it handles the difficult aspects, this book should earn special merit for the writers. Abortion, as Liebman and Zimmer point out, and as Ney and Feldmar confirm, is the test of a truly concerned society—a society with a healing vision, affirming life and wanting to help.

The writers are in basic agreement concerning the need to think in terms of alternatives to abortion. A profession which employs a single modality of treatment such as abortion to a situation amenable to others has simply boxed itself in and shows an alarming lack of imagination. Society, the writers maintain, should protect pregnant women through a strong and reliable support system. Psychiatry should give hope and banish despair as its contribution to the total effort. The answer to the negativism of abortion is to be found in a caring society.

Without question, abortion is psychologically a symbol of the despair which seems to be endemic in modern society. It is a totally negative response to environmental pressures. Without benefit of an affirming love, abortion is always an empty response—a gesture of denial as characterized by Baars in his essay.

This book stresses what good doctors and scientists should be doing to put the abortion question in perspective. Out of the sea of conjecture surrounding the psychological aspects of abortion emerges the somewhat heretical idea that social policy may have moved in the wrong direction. The writers challenge the heretofore sacrosanct assumption that carrying an unwanted child to term is more traumatic than abortion. They assert that, instead of abdicating to the abortionist, the best interest of the patient is served by treating the patient's psychological problems.

Whatever final disposition society (and medicine) may make of the abortion question, the facts advanced in this book will have to be considered. They cannot be ignored; nor can they be assim-

---

* During the symposium, an in-depth study of Ian Kent of Vancouver, B.C., was widely quoted. The study involved over fifty postabortive women in psychotherapy who revealed painful feelings of profound regret; indeed, it was later discovered that very few of these women would willingly have another abortion. Kent's findings were in sharp contrast to the standard questionnaire survey results of postabortive women which heretofore have led policy makers to conclude that abortion is likely to produce no seriously adverse emotional consequences. See *BC Medical Journal*, XX, No. 4, April 1978, pp. 118-9.

ilated without further investigation, and a radical rethinking of social policy. Reasoning from known evidence, the essays provide some of the key data needed to refashion our thinking.

In the final analysis, what this book suggests is that life is better than death, and that psychotherapy which affirms life is by far the best. Abortion is a defeatist answer, a psychic retreat for those who have given up looking for answers.

Where will this book lead? The editors hope that it will open new avenues of investigation among behavioral scientists, physicians, and health care professionals, and will stimulate a new awareness among the discerning general public. We are a society in need of a genuine healing approach to our most critical social problems. Toward that end, this book is a beginning.

Post-Abortive Psychoses:
A Report from Two Centers

Myre Sim, M.D.
and
Robert Neisser, M.D.

That post-abortive psychoses do occur is not seriously questioned. Since Ekblad[1] reported that 2 percent had severe psychiatric sequelae in 479 abortions on psychiatric grounds, others have tried to estimate the precise incidence, but a true estimate is still elusive.

There are reasons for this. Much of the evidence has been based on hospital admissions, yet this can be a very unreliable method. In modern urban societies, where adequate out-patient facilities exist, severe psychiatric morbidity can be satisfactorily treated on an out-patient or day-hospital basis; so many, if not most such patients, would not be recorded if admission to hospital were the sole criterion. Furthermore, it would be more likely, because of the infant, that a post-partum psychosis would, if at all possible, be treated on an out-patient basis. These considerations make the estimate of Jansen[2] of 19.2 per 1000 legal abortions and 2.7 per 1000 for illegal and spontaneous abortions less than reliable, as would the incidence of 0.2-0.4 per 1000 in a series of 73,000 legal abortions after a short follow-up (Tietze and Lewit[3]). The larger figure would be nearer the truth though how near is not possible to say.

If the incidence of post-abortive psychoses is no greater than that of post-partum psychoses, one would expect an incidence of 1 per 800-1000. This illustrates the unreliability of many of the statistically validated and controlled studies, one of the largest being that of McCance et al.[4] which compared 186 "controls" who were refused abortion with 123 who had a therapeutic abortion. It drew the conclusion that because the incidence of psychiatric sequelae was about equal, abortion presented no greater psychiatric hazard than pregnancy. To make this observation valid, there would have to be no less than 10,000 subjects a side. Yet, in spite of the very large number of abortions in recent years, such a study has not been undertaken and one may legitimately wonder why it has not been done.

A more recent study by Brewer[5] was based on a questionnaire addressed to practicing psychiatrists in the West Midlands of England. He reported over a period of 15 months an incidence of post-abortive psychoses of 0.3 per 1000, but the study was flawed in many respects. Specifically, only 25 percent of the psychiatrists participated; the criterion of morbidity was hospital admission; his comparison with post-partum psychoses also depended on hospital admission; and the psychiatrist with the greatest responsibility and experience in the area of the assessment and treatment of patients with instability associated with pregnancy did not participate.

One may never know the true incidence of post-abortive psychoses but there are good grounds for assuming that it is much higher than the estimates of Tietze and Lewit[3] and of Brewer.[5] It may not be higher than that following childbirth, though in selected groups such as those who have an abortion because of previous psychiatric illness, it would be much higher.

Dr. Sim, since 1951, has been particularly interested in the problem of instability associated with pregnancy. Intimately associated for 24 years as a psychiatrist with the Department of Obstetrics and Gynaecology of the University of Birmingham, England, he was in a favorable position to pursue his research. This interest was stimulated by a particular patient, who, having had 18 months previously, a severe post-partum schizophrenic illness from which she had not recovered, was again pregnant, and the question of a therapeutic abortion was raised. In 1951 such a problem was regarded as a classical indication for termination. This recommendation was made but was surprisingly rejected by the patient. She was therefore allowed to continue with her pregnancy, and to everybody's surprise she improved mentally and maintained this improvement after delivery and on subsequent long-term follow-up.

It was obvious that psychiatric recommendations for abortion were not based on sound evidence and were no more than guesswork determined by mythology and social customs. There was much to learn. The lesson from this patient started a 12-year study of 213 patients who had experienced a post-partum psychosis. Its lack of predictability, the good prognosis, the remarkably low incidence of suicide during pregnancy, and a large number of other factors were reported by Dr. Sim[6] in 1963. The conclusions were that abortion had no place in the treatment of the mentally ill or, for that matter, in the prevention of mental illness.

As a conservative policy towards abortion was adopted from the start, a larger body of information on instability associated with pregnancy, including the psychiatric sequelae following abortion, was collected and analyzed, the total number of patients being 482.

During this time, Dr. Neisser came to Birmingham from Israel as a Wolfson Research Fellow and developed an interest in the work which he pursued on his return. The results of these two studies in regard to post-abortive psychoses are now presented.

The Birmingham Study

A total of 56 patients were treated for post-abortive psychoses and the effect of the greater number of abortions done just prior to and after the passing of the Abortion Act, 1967, is reflected in Table 1.

Table 1
Post-Abortive Psychoses

	Therapeutic	Spontaneous and Criminal	Total
1950-1963	4	4	8
1964-1975	38	10	48
			56

If post-abortive psychoses could be used as an index of the number of abortions, there would appear to have been a marked rise in abortions. Too much should not be read into the relatively small increase in psychoses following spontaneous and criminal abortions. It is likely that anybody with a history of instability could qualify for a therapeutic abortion and would therefore not seek a criminal one, and it is now well established that a previous history of mental illness predisposes to a post-abortive psychosis. It does cast serious doubt on the claim that the Abortion Act has not resulted in more abortions but has merely shifted the criminal and spontaneous to the therapeutic.

A disturbing feature of the post-abortive psychoses study was that four of these patients who had been refused an abortion on psychiatric grounds but had elected to have one eventually, were referred later with a severe post-abortive psychosis. This raises the issue of refusing abortion, which in some circles has been regarded as a reactionary and moralistic attitude. Yet there is now enough evidence to show that where there was a previous history of mental illness, a so-called "therapeutic" abortion can be dangerous.

We had the other experience of patients who had a previous abortion with a resultant post-abortive psychosis who again became pregnant and were allowed to go to term. In the majority of instances no post-partum psychosis resulted (Table 2).

Table 2

Post-Abortive Psychoses	Post-Partum Psychoses	Total
12	3	15

Prognosis in Post-Abortive Psychoses

While much consideration is given to the incidence of post-abortive psychoses, little attention has been paid to prognosis. No doctor would willingly expose his patient to a mental illness, but if it could be shown that one therapeutic approach carried a good prognosis and the other a poor prognosis, it would be of great assistance in arriving at a decision as to whether to abort (Table 3).

Table 3

Prognosis

	Number	Good Prognosis	Poor Prognosis
Post-Partum Psychoses	311	307	4
Post-Abortive Psychoses	56	28	28

A good prognosis is defined as a good response to treatment with full remission of symptoms and restoration to the pre-morbid level of functioning and in an acceptable time, without the problem of a relapsing course. A poor prognosis would omit one or all of these features.

Not all psychiatric sequelae following abortion are so florid that they must be referred to a general psychiatric clinic. Kent,[7] at the Annual Meeting of the Canadian Psychiatric Association in September, 1977, in Saskatoon, reported on 30 patients who were in psychotherapy. It was only in the course of therapy that they declared that the major precipitating factor in their problem and a continuing factor in its prolongation was a previous abortion. Furthermore, these same patients, when given a questionnaire, did not admit to the abortion being the key factor in their disability. This casts doubt on the value of questionnaires or the standard follow-up in such patients. This has also been reported by Casselman[8] in her capacity as director of a student mental health service.

In a society where abortion is virtually on demand, a psychiatrist who prefers to use his expertise to treat psychiatric problems rather than refer them to the gynecologist will not have large numbers of patients referred for abortion. Yet a total of 67 were referred for this purpose (Table 4).

Table 4

Refused Abortion

Satisfactory Outcome (Mother and Child)		54 (80.6%)
Aborted		5 (7.4%)
Not Traced		8 (12.0%)
	Total	67 (100.0%)

Previous Abortion	9
Previous Post-Partum Psychoses	18
Other Psychiatric Illness	23
Family History of Mental Illness	13

Of those who accepted the advice to continue to term (80.6 percent of the total), all had a satisfactory outcome. Unfortunately, the inability to follow up the rest did not permit comparison. This is a common problem, for it is much more difficult to follow up abortions than pregnancies. The presence of the baby makes the event public and there is no possibility of, or advantage in, concealment. With abortion there is the intention by all concerned to turn it into a non-event, and in many instances attempt at follow-up is regarded as an impertinence if not a betrayal.

The Israeli Study

From the demographic standpoint it is not possible to say how many post-abortive psychoses occur in Israel, but there are indications that they are not uncommon.

During a 3-year period at a government psychiatric hospital out-patient department, 58 women in the course of their first psychiatric interview volunteered the information that abortion (induced or spontaneous) led to their referral to the psychiatric clinic. There were some patients who, in subsequent interviews or after direct questioning, did admit to abortion being a factor in their problem, but these were not included in this study.

All the induced abortions occurred in the first trimester and the spontaneous abortions occurred in the first-second trimesters. Of the 58 cases, 55 were married, two who had previously been diagnosed as schizophrenic were unmarried, and one was a widow. One of the married women with severe depression had conceived extramaritally. Table 5 illustrates the type of abortion and post-abortion breakdown.

Table 5

Type of Abortion and Type of Post-Abortive Breakdown

Diagnosis	Spontaneous	Induced	Total
Schizophrenic Reaction	1	11	12
Acute Psychotic Reaction	—	5	5
Affective Psychosis (Depression)	8	14	22
Neurotic Reaction (Acute Anxiety)	5	14	19
Total	14	44	58

"Acute psychotic reaction" referred to those patients with their first acute psychotic episode even if it showed schizophrenic and paranoid features. All schizophrenic reactions were of the process type. Twenty patients in all had a previous history of psychiatric illness, of which six were post-partum psychoses, but abortion did not prevent a relapse. All the other 38 women who had a clear history required psychiatric treatment after abortion.

Fifteen women with a history of previous mental illness requiring psychiatric treatment had previously given birth to one or more children without developing a post-partum psychosis or severe neurotic disability, but did so following abortion. Of the total of 58 patients seen initially on an out-patient basis, 9 were admitted to a psychiatric hospital for treatment.

Seven women who had post-abortive psychoses subsequently became pregnant again, went to term and suffered no adverse psychiatric sequelae. One woman was pregnant with her fourteenth child and was persuaded by her physician to have an abortion on social grounds and reacted with a severe psychotic depression, made a very determined attempt at suicide and narrowly escaped death.

Of the 58 women, 7 made serious attempts at suicide and another three threatened suicide. This must give serious concern as to whether, in unstable women, the suicidal risk is in fact greater following abortion than after pregnancy.

Discussion

These 114 instances of severe mental illness following abortion do not tell us anything about the incidence of the problem. Some critics may even dismiss the two series as "anecdotal" because they do not state the population at risk, i.e., the total number of abortions performed and the cultural and other factors which may have predisposed these women. The inability to submit the data to a full statistical analysis would also be criticized and in anticipation of these criticisms we would like to place our data in a proper perspective.

Clinical medicine owes its origins and its growth almost entirely to "anecdote." From earlier times until the present, clinical medicine has advanced on "anecdote" whether the raconteur was Aesculpius, Maimonides, Avicenna, Sydenham, or the spate of physicians who describe eponymous diseases like Addison's disease, Bright's disease, Parkinson's disease, Huntington's disease, and the like. There is not a single disease in the medical dictionary which did not see light of day as an "anecdote," or to be more exact, as the result of a doctor's observations. Furthermore, there is not a single disease in the medical dictionary which achieved recognition through statistical validation. In fact, if this were the criterion of acceptance, most diseases would be shown to be nonexistent, other than those in wards of hospitals or on death certificates.

Epidemiology, which treats of whole populations, relies on statistical methods. Clinical medicine does not need to rely on averages; in fact, as Claude Bernard said, "the true relation of phenomena disappear in the average."[9]

It is now recognized that even a meticulously planned and statistically validated clinical trial of a new drug will not detect all its dangerous side effects. This often has to wait for the "anecdotal" reports of individual physicians. It was in this way that the embryopathic effects of Thalidomide were discovered and the corneal damage from Practolol. We therefore consider that we are following in the time-honored medical tradition of reporting the undesirable sequelae of a treatment which has gained rapidly in popularity and which is being promoted by some as being perfectly safe and, in fact, safer than pregnancy.

We have produced evidence that abortion does precipitate severe mental illness, particularly in vulnerable women but by no means exclusively. The onset of the illness can be similar to a post-partum psychosis, i.e., from 6-12 weeks after the abortion, so that any conclusions drawn from immediate reactions to the operation can be very fallacious. The reports by Kent[7] and Casselman[8] indicate that there are many less florid but nevertheless disabling sequelae from abortion which are being ignored by those who advocate the operation.

The prognosis of a post-abortion psychosis is a material consideration. If, as we have demonstrated, the post-partum psychosis carries an excellent prognosis and the post-abortive psychosis carries a relatively poor one, argument about incidence even if based on valid data has very little place. If these lessons would be taken to heart, at least those most vulnerable, namely, those with a previous history of instability, could be spared the risk of prolonged disability. It should also give grounds for concern to those who recommend abortion in the hope of preventing mental illness, when there is now considerable evidence that the very measure which is intended to benefit the patient can precipitate the patient into a worse state than if she were allowed to go to term.

Doctors who adopt a conservative approach to abortion have been attacked and even legislated against. They are accused of imposing their morality on the patient and told that their attitude is an unsympathetic one in that they are placing their own moral stance above the patient's best interests. Apart from the issue that a pregnancy presents a doctor with two patients and that the fetus is entitled to every consideration, there are other medical issues that cannot be dismissed as dogma or religious conscience. There is the matter of a medical conscience which demands that a doctor should act in his patient's best interests.

Furthermore, it has been said that to refuse to abort is a banishment of the patient who is left to fend for herself as best she may. Nothing could be further from the truth. Refusal to abort implies an undertaking to look after the patient so that she can have her baby in safety. This is reflected in the follow-up of patients who accept such advice, which is 100 percent. It must be a very unusual form of banishment which is underwritten by such a commitment. In an unstable person there is always the risk, albeit slight, of a post-partum psychosis but here again, the experienced psychiatrist can undertake this with confidence in the knowledge that with abortion the risk is greater, certainly in terms of prognosis.

If abortion is considered to be a procedure which has no undesirable sequelae for pregnant women and can be undertaken with impunity, though the facts presented demonstrate the opposite, then the debate for those who are so inclined can be channelled into the question of the mother's convenience versus the rights of the fetus.

We do not imply in any way the rights of the fetus should be sacrificed, but would add that the rights of the mother to the best medical treatment should also be borne in mind. Our studies show that abortion is bad treatment for mental illness and for its prevention, and doctors who refuse to use it for such purposes are acting in their patient's best interests. When one considers that upwards of 95 percent of abortions are done on psychiatric grounds, it is very odd indeed that those physicians who advocate such abortions should feel that they are practicing a better brand of medicine. We hope that our report will reinforce the resolve of those who have maintained their professional integrity, and stimulate those who have not, to see that they have been victims of a propaganda machine which has paraded untruth and disregarded valid evidence.

Medical Ethics and the Law

One must again inquire as to why, in the face of this information we present, which is not unique in psychiatric experience, the leaders of the medical profession in countries which have passed permissive abortion laws have in general supported these laws. In the United Kingdom when the medical termination of pregnancy bill became law as the Abortion Act of 1967, the General Medical Council, which is the body regulating the registration and conduct of medical practitioners, wrote immediately to the *British Medical Journal* that as abortion on certain grounds was now legal, doctors who aborted under the provisions of the new Act could not be charged as before with serious professional misconduct.

This raises the important distinction between what is legal and what is medically ethical. Governments pass many, perhaps too many, laws.

Some are good and some are bad; some are lasting and some are hastily withdrawn or amended. The medical profession has a clear duty to ignore those laws that are counter to medical ethics, even if by doing so it courts the full rigor of the law. The Nuremburg Laws of the Nazis contained a number of such instances and those doctors who kept faith with their medical ethics were praised, even if posthumously, while those who did not have been brought to trial or are still being hunted as war criminals.

A disturbing feature of the present craze for abortion on demand and the acquiescence of the medical profession, is that serious studies to arrive at the truth have not been undertaken so that laws were passed on little or no evidence. With the British Act, the pro-life groups adopted a course of scientific detachment, confident that the facts, if available, would prove them right and give them not less than 99 percent of their demands in terms of abortions performed. They therefore asked that before Parliament enacted legislation, there should be a Royal Commission to inquire into the facts so that both Parliament and the public could be informed. This was hastily brushed aside, for the abortion law reformers had decided that the time for the Act was opportune and that delay could forfeit their advantage.

This may be acceptable as far as the political process is concerned but when a measure such as an abortion act is being contemplated, one has a right to expect that responsible government would see that this was fundamental to the structure of society itself, that it affects respect for life itself, and that it therefore ought not to have been pushed through on a wave of propaganda based on half-truths and untruths. Many misguided people were persuaded by the arguments. Numbers were exaggerated more than tenfold. In the United Kingdom it was claimed that 500,000 illegal abortions a year were being performed. Now, it is estimated that figure was more like 25,000. The Act was designed to get rid of illegal abortions but most of the evidence from various countries shows that very little impact is made. Of course, if you start with a grossly inflated number it is very easy to say, when a proper estimate has been made, that the difference is due to the Act.

If the law makes an act more legal for one section of the community, in this case, doctors, it cannot make it more illegal for another section, the illegal abortionists. They take their cue from the local medical practice. If this practice is permissive then, even if apprehended, their chances of being convicted are much less. After all, they are doing the same thing for the same reasons as the doctors and for a smaller fee. It would be a very poor attorney, armed with this information, who could not convince a jury that his client was more to be congratulated than condemned. The act of abortion itself is no longer illegal, only the practitioner. If local medical practice is conservative, the situation is very different. In this case the illegal abortionist is much more cautious, for he knows that if apprehended he would be faced by medical specialists who would swear on oath that they would never, under similar circumstances, perform an abortion, and had never in fact done so.

This sounds right, but is there any evidence to support this? Dr. Sim, who worked in Birmingham, England, where a conservative policy was in operation, in spite of the Abortion Act, was accosted by a gynecologist who had come there from Manchester where a more permissive medical attitude was prevalent. He was puzzled. The propagandists had told him that in a city like Birmingham the illegal abortion rate would be very high; yet the index he used, namely, the admission of the incomplete abortions, was very much lower than in Manchester. The answer was obvious. By making an act more legal for one section of society, one does not make it more illegal for another. Similarly, the private abortion clinic in the city drew a substantial number of its patients from outside the city, and many came from far afield. The reason was that the local medical practitioners knew that their specialists in gynecology and psychiatry were acting in their patients' best interests and were content to support their decisions.

Another argument put forward was that under the old system, only the rich could get an abortion through medical channels while the poor had to be content with the illegal abortionist. Whenever the poor are expected to compete for services with the well-to-do, there is one thing which is certain. They go to the end of a longer queue. But there is another and more sinister aspect. Many see the Abortion Act as a means of controlling the number of the under-privileged. Just as an inadequate psychiatrist resorts to abortion when psychiatric competence can insure a better result, so many social workers invoke the gynecologist's assistance for what are basically social problems. It is not surprising that the Third World rejects this arbitrary attitude toward their offspring and that the under-privileged minority groups in the U.S.A. see these measures as threatening and demeaning.

Abortion, it was claimed, would eliminate the mental sequelae of pregnancy. These are, in severe degrees, very rare and occur in the region of 1 in 800-1000 live births, so the prediction of their occurrence is extremely difficult. Even when the indices are heavily loaded, there is not more than a 20 percent chance of this happening. It is also now clear that when there is a prospect of such an event, abortion is strongly contraindicated, so the "mental" argument has no basis as an indication for abortion. Yet psychiatrists and others are still recommending abortions on psychiatric grounds. The psychiatric argument is being exploited to gain more room to maneuver, for in our permissive society there is still the need to obtain the blessing of the new priesthood, the medical profession.

Since the passing of the Abortion Act there has been a furious search for justification, and through totally inadequate and flawed sampling, poor follow-up, and a failure to search for and note the psychiatric sequelae of abortion, the myth has been propagated that abortion is safer than pregnancy. Mentally, it is not, and physically the comparisons are uneven. The vast majority of abortions are done on fit young women while pregnancy is frequently undertaken by women of all ages, many of whom have a physical illness which makes their pregnancy a hazard. In these women the baby is wanted and they are prepared to take the risk.

This again highlights the danger of "averaging" information. This method insures that the truth is dissolved in the average. The present obsession with statistical validation has brought us to the stage that no study can achieve scientific respectability unless it is upholstered by a sufficiency of elegant algebra. An aphorism of the late Lord Kelvin that "all science is measurement" has been distorted to read that "all measurement is science." Nothing could be further from the truth. Statistics or averaging is a certain way of concealing or distorting the truth, particularly where clinical phenomena are concerned. This does not mean that the clinician should not pay due regard to method in his experiment and accuracy in his reporting, but he is unlikely to extract the truth by the lumping together of numbers and subjecting them to statistical analysis. Some of the classical diseases whose descriptions have stood the test of centuries were based on accurate observation on one case.

Another claim of the pro-abortionist was that an unwanted pregnancy was a common cause of suicide and indeed this was frequently given as the justification of abortion. Dr. Sim specifically inquired into this and found that in a 12-year period in Birmingham, England, a city with a population of 1,250,000, there was only one case of suicide in a pregnant woman and in her case the question of abortion was never raised.[6] The woman was married, was mentally ill, and was in fact attending a psychiatric clinic at the time. This information was initially hotly disputed and the argument was adulterated with figures for attempted suicide, but the general conclusion still holds. A pregnant woman is less likely to commit suicide than her matched sister who is not pregnant. Rather interestingly, once she has given birth, the risk of suicide rises to the average. The data from Israel would also suggest that if the pregnancy is aborted the risk rises considerably. A psychiatrist published a paper in the *Lancet* several years ago claiming, on the basis of a small series, that he had seen no psychiatric sequelae from abortion. The following week a gynecologist, no doubt with tongue-in-cheek, reported that he had a patient who had suicided after abortion but that this was really a physical rather than a psychiatric sequel to abortion.

Medical ethics as enshrined in the Hipprocratic oath even antedates Christianity, so doctors need not be concerned with religious dogma. We have a duty to act in the best interests of our patients, the born and the unborn. It may be presumptuous of us to say so, but we believe that in adhering to these ethics we would not incur the displeasure of any of the world's great religions.

References

1. Ekblad, M. 1955. Induced abortion on psychiatric grounds. *Acta Psychiat. Neurol. Scand.* Suppl. 99:1.
2. Jansson, B. 1965. Mental disorders after abortion. *Acta Psyciat. Scand.* 41: 87.
3. Tietze, C., and Lewit, S. 1972. Joint program for the study of abortion (JPSA): Earlier medical complications of legal abortion. *Studies in Family Planning.* 3: 97.
4. McCance, C.; Olley, P.C.; and Edward, V. 1973. Overall Clinical Psychiatric Assessment. In G. Horobin, ed. *Experience with Abortion.* London: Cambridge University Press.
5. Brewer, C. 1977. Medicine of post-abortion psychosis: a prospective study. *Brit. Med. J.* 1: 476-477.
6. Sim, M. 1963. Abortion and the psychiatrist. *Brit. Med. J.* 2: 145-148.
7. Kent, I. 1977. Emotional sequelae of therapeutic abortion. Paper presented to the 27th Annual Meeting of the Canadian Psychiatric Association in Saskatoon, September 1977.
8. Casselman, J. 1978. Personal communication.
9. Bernard, C. 1865. *Introduction a l'etude de la medicine experimentale.* Balliere, Paris.

The Embryology of Consciousness: What Is a Normal Pregnancy?

Andrew Feldmar, Ph.D.

Introduction

> Once there was a poor orphan with no one to teach him either his way, or his manners. Sometimes animals helped him, sometimes supernatural beings. But above all, one thing was evident. Unlike other occupants of Earth he had to be helped. He did not know his place, he had to find it. Sometimes he was arrogant and had to learn humility, sometimes he was a coward and had to be taught bravery. Sometimes he did not understand his Mother Earth and suffered for it. The old ones who starved and sought visions on hilltops had known these things. They were all gone now and the magic had departed with them. The orphan was alone; he had to learn by himself; it was a hard school.[1]

I am acutely aware of being this cosmic orphan as I write this essay; I am riddled with doubt, misgivings, and ignorance. I am a skeptic (i.e., an inquirer, always unsatisfied, yet always looking and yearning for truth), wondering what's "good," what's "bad"; what to do, what not to do.

The meaning of this essay is the action it will produce. Knowledge, by itself, cannot originate action; its function is to direct the action that is initiated and maintained by feeling and will. Feeling and will are moved, in their turn, by a philosophy of life and also, to some extent, by the detailed knowledge of what might be expected to happen if a certain course of action were adopted.[2] What

Plato meant when he said, "No one can do wrong voluntarily," becomes clear in the light of something else he said: "Ignorance is the greatest evil." This logic implies an optimistic view of man: Replace ignorance with awareness and knowledge and the right actions will be taken. Thomas Szasz, in a more cynical mood, suggests that if in the service of evil we are hell-bent on doing harm, we *must* remain ignorant, we simply cannot afford to expand our awareness. My aims in writing this essay are the following:

1. To make a case for the statement, "The origin of consciousness, sentience, i.e., the beginning of one's relevant lifetime, must be dated at conception, if not before."

2. To explore some of the implications of the above statement when we think of abortion, pre-, and peri-natal care.

3. To ask questions that cut through the great taboo of immediacy; questions that cannot be answered in the abstract, but have to be faced alone by each one of us before we can do more than pretend to know where we stand on certain critical issues.

The Statement and Its Implications

In 1642, Sir Thomas Browne wrote in his *Religio Medici*:

> And surely we are all out of the computation of our age, and every man is some months elder than he bethinks him; for we live, move, have a being, and are subject to the actions of the elements, and the malice of diseases, in that other World, the truest Microcosm, the Womb of our Mother.

My beginnings are contained in the zygote that formed in my mother's uterine tube at the moment her ovum fused with my father's sperm. I still carry, in every single cell of my body, the same genetic code that emerged during that moment of fusion. My interaction with my environment also began at that precise moment. R. D. Laing suggests the possibility that one's impact, influence, effect on the environment may be at a never-to-be surpassed maximum during the days after conception. Elaborate, intricate and long-lasting changes take place in that vast community of cells I will later learn to call mother, as a direct response to my arrival. Women who have learned to pay attention to their dreams can often pinpoint the time they conceived from the unmistakable content of a dream that occurred no more than a few hours after coitus. The news travels fast.

Alexander Maven[4] speculates that human gametes are capable of experiencing the event of union and of recording that experience so that it can be "played back." This "playback," Maven argues, is the basis of the mystical experience of spiritual union with God or the Divine. Across cultures and throughout time, mystics have reported basically three varieties of experiencing such a union: (a) the Divine spirit enters the soul and uniting with it transforms and immortalizes it; (b) the soul or self enters the Divine to dissolve and merge with it; (c) the soul both is entered by and enters the Divine. It's exciting to correlate these varieties with the kind of playback one would expect from the ovum's, the sperm's, and the zygote's point of view.

Mythologists and anthropologists often wondered what might account for the seemingly independent emergence of certain themes, configurations, images, and symbols in the myths, legends, and fairy tales of people widely separated in time and space. C. G. Jung invented the concept of a "collective, universal unconscious" to explain such phenomena, as well as to account for the equally puzzling occurrences of ancient symbols in the dreams and hallucinations of his modern patients.

Following the lead of Francis Mott,[4] Otto Rank,[5] Nandor Fodor,[6] R. D. Laing,[7] and Stanislav Grof,[8] it must be postulated that myths, fairy tales, legends, dreams, visions, and hallucinations can be expressions of vivid memories of certain pre-, or peri-natal experiences. All of us, members of the species *Homo sapiens*, regardless of place or time, of culture or race, have almost identical beginnings. Our early environment, mother's womb, and the major events in that environment (fertilization, cleavage, blastulation, implantation, placentation, gastrulation, growth and differentiation, and finally parturition) have been our common lot, our shared, universal experience.

For example, consider the story of Moses (Exodus 2). He is born into a dangerous environment since "Pharaoh charged all his people, saying, Every son that is born ye shall cast into the river." Let's take his parents, an ordinary Levi couple, to be the sperm and egg that formed the zygote (i.e., Moses) which during its first seven or eight days of life is perhaps most in danger of extinction. The river in whose waters his parents abandoned him, floating in an "ark of bullrushes, daubed with slime and with pitch" (the zona pellucida) could be thought of as the uterine tube that takes about seven or eight days to navigate. Out of its waters, Pharaoh's daughter adopts Moses to be her son. This idea of second parenting by royalty occurs in many myths and is characteristic of the origin of the hero. The accomplishment of the blastula to gain entry into the mother's endometrium (implantation) seems analogous to Moses' accomplishment of finding a royal protector under whose wings his survival is assured. Had he been left floating by the river's side, among the flags and bullrushes, he would have perished, just as blastulas perish that cannot gain entry into the lining of the womb.

Laing and Grof both agree that the earlier in a person's development interaction with the environment becomes traumatic, the more serious will be the nature of later personality and psychological disturbances. The origin of psychoses seems to be pre- or perinatal. The origin of neuroses seems to be later, in infancy or early childhood. My mother's uterus may have been welcoming, nourishing and protective, or it could have been poisonous, stressful, and hostile to me. Many womb environments may not be optimal for the genetic response system that is built into the growing fetus. Mother's womb cannot be assumed to be a positive environment. In the U.S.A. alone, it is estimated that more than 1.2 million abortions are carried out per year! Even the earliest environmental impressions may create a reverberating echo in all the cells that have descended from the one, and now constitute the colony of millions I call myself.

From the moment of conception I am exposed to danger. My encounters with the environment may not lead to death, but far from optimal stress seems to leave its imprint deep inside my cells. If my first interpenetrating contact with the host tissue (endometrium) is conjunctive, i.e., I am welcomed, accepted as if into a "bed of crimson joy," this positive first impression of how I am received may color all my subsequent impressions of entering with anticipation, hope, and excitement. If, however, that first contact turns out to be disjunctive, i.e., I am resisted and attacked as an invading tissue by my mother's immune system, and I have to enter by force, like the marines landing at the enemy's beachhead, this negative first impression may color subsequent entries with fear, hostility, and grim determination.

The womb becomes a tomb. If we fail to get buried (implanted) we never get born. Hence all the myths of death and rebirth. Placentation is the blueprint for Eve's creation out of Adam. My placenta was my double, my twin, my incestuous lover (e.g., Isis and Osiris). The importance of these early months cannot be overstressed. Psychological time gets longer as we move towards our origin, shorter as we move towards adulthood. The intrauterine processes thus seem to last for an eternity and impress themselves on us indelibly.

Last year I was guest speaker at Medical Rounds in a major hospital in British Colulmbia. I could hardly believe my ears when the head of obstetrics began talking about "the mother's placenta." It may at first seem like splitting hairs to point out that by the time a woman gives birth she has surely lost *her* placenta. The obstetrician meant, "the newborn's placenta." The slip, however, reveals a mental set that determines one's attitudes and actions. As long as I think of the placenta as the mother's, I don't have to feel sympathy for the newborn when I cut the cord. It wouldn't occur to me that I just amputated a sentient being who is in the midst of the most horrendous biological trauma. Leboyer's[9] tender caring would make little sense to one who never realized that for what must have felt like eons, "I" was the experience of the throbbing and pulsing of *my* blood in *my* body, made up of the trinity of "placenta—umbilical cord—fetus." This obstetrician couldn't possibly have conceived of the idea that the newborn may have a vivid experience of a "phantom placenta" (cf. the "phantom limb" experience of amputees). In fantasy, then, the following mappings can take place, just to mention a few:

	placenta	cord	fetus
	lung	neck	head
or	breast	nipple/ mouth	body of baby
or	woman	penis	man

The trauma of the prematurely cut cord can be healed, *nursed*, by a satisfactory feeding experience. If weaning is again traumatic, the terror associated with CUTTING will be reinforced. Disturbances in eating, breathing, metabolism, relationships and _ ital function can originate right here. Sex may be continually sought to re-establish the throb and pulse of pre-natal experience—our amputated half trying to find its lost "better" half.

To summarize, I view my present, adult experience as built on and profoundly influenced and colored by my earliest encounters with my environment. Serious confusion of pre- and post-natal life is incompatible with sanity. If I fail to recognize that what I am afraid of has already happened, I may live in terror long after the danger has passed. The aim of all psychotherapy has to be a release from the spell of past catastrophies. What is a normal pregnancy? From conception until I find myself for the first time nursing on my mother's breast, I encounter a series of different environments (uterine tube, endometrium, womb, breast); if I survive these encounters without death, injury, illness, or other catastrophic experiences that could lead to psychic helplessness— then pregnancy was normal. Otherwise, I will be in need of a healer.

The great difficulty is that physical traumas can be detected minutes after birth, whereas psychic traumas might not surface for years. The Apgar Scoring Chart, which is used in all Vancouver hospitals, cannot detect the newborn's psychological condition. The obstetric and pediatric community is preoccupied with the child's physiological condition.

Three doctors, on nationwide television in 1976, commented on Leboyer's "birth without violence," uttering phrases such as the following: "unnecessary," "no harm done by current practice," "99 percent of all deliveries are optimal," "no visible problem in the delivery room, so why innovate?" I must point out the irony of the word "visible." Two hundred years of puerperal fever came to an end twenty years after Ignaz Philipp Semmelweis,[10] a Hungarian physician, first suggested that these deaths were iatrogenic. In 1861 he published a passionate plea to compel all physicians to wash their hands in chlorinated lime on entering a labor room. Semmelweis' findings, and his polemics against doctors and clinics, met with such antagonism that he was professionally discredited and for twenty years his simple prescription was totally ignored. After four years of futile battle, Semmelweis was committed to the Vienna Insane Asylum, where he died soon after. The doctors wanted *visible* proof. So they waited for Pasteur's demonstration of the reality of bacterial infection. Semmelweis' demonstration that in his clinic, shortly after instituting a strict regime of hand-washing, the death rate fell drastically, was ignored. Not out of malice, I think, but due to a failure to conceive the connections; all the more so, since seeing the connection would have meant recognizing the physician's part in the tragedy. To quote Semmelweis, "I must here confess that God only knows the number of patients that have gone prematurely to their graves by my fault." I can only hope we will not wait for the discovery of the exact biochemical processes involved in our pre-and peri-natal sensitivity, memory and reactivity, before adopting Leboyer's prescriptions. I am reminded of Max Planck's sad remark, "A new scientific truth does not triumph by convincing its opponents and making them see the light, but rather because its opponents eventually die, and a new generation grows up that is familiar with it."

Mankind's survival may depend on learning to attend to connections, patterns, and causalities that are not obvious because of the time that elapses between cause and effect. I am talking about the relatively new science of ecology. If I pull the trigger, aiming my gun at you and you fall down and die, it's easy to see what's cause and what's effect. The effect of dumping garbage into the ocean has escaped us until recently. Even now it's not easy to effectively remind and compel individual members of our species to alter present behavior in order to avoid a calamity in the future.

The topic of this conference, abortion, is really such an eco-logical issue. Most people do not engage in sex because they want a child; they have sex for pleasure.[11] In the heat of passion we re-sist taking responsibility for a possible future calamity (i.e., un-wanted pregnancy, abortion, etc.).

Leboyer, the last I heard, is in no danger of following in Sem-melweis' footsteps. I think of him, too, as an ecologist. He, along with Laing, Grof, and others, pleads with us to consider the effects of the very early environment (pre- and peri-natal) on later (ten, twenty, thirty years later!) personality development.

In my own work, I discovered that an unsuccessful attempt at abortion can be remembered (unconsciously) by the child and much later commemorated by repeated and unsuccessful suicide attempts. Even the style of the suicide echoes the style of the abortion (i.e., mother used mechanical means, so did the child; mother used a chemical, child tried to overdose). The time be-tween the two events may be thirty years or more. Neither mother nor child makes the connection. Until asked, mother may have never confessed to anyone her early assassination attempt, least of all to her child. Once the connection is made, the child is relieved of compulsively having to act out a memory. What seemed like insanity turns out to be a haunting memory. Thomas Szasz[12] writes, "If you start out with a big lie, it doesn't matter how many truths you add to it, the result will be more lies." Cop-outs for difficult moral questions rest on lies. One such cop-out is to treat human conflicts, life problems, as if they were diseases. Neither the decision to ask for nor the decision to perform an abortion are medical problems. Legal, perhaps; but not medical. A women who is suffering from the "sequelae of abortion" is like a soldier who is sickened by the memory of his own killing of the enemy, or even more, she is like a survivor of Hiroshima, feeling guilty for having survived in the midst of the carnage.

Nothing but the truth will be therapeutically effective. The concept of "quickening" as a point after which a fetus is human, before which it is a malignant growth, or any other such arbitrary point is clearly an invention in the service of repression and denial and therefore is pathogenic.

David Bakan,[13] in his brilliant book on the battered child phe-nomenon, asks:

> If the man-woman-child "holy trinity" is a kind of
> ultimate paradigm of wholeness, wholesomeness,
> and holiness, what then corresponds to sin? I came
> to believe that the answer must be infanticide, the
> killing of the new life that results from the coming

together of the male and the female. The crushing out of the life of a child is, in my opinion, the most heinous of all crimes.

Questions

1. Is it possible that the fruit of the tree of knowledge which Adam and Eve ate was a fetus and therefore they were the first couple to perform an abortion? Is abortion the original sin? The word "knowing" means also "sexual intercourse" in the Bible. The fruit of knowledge is therefore a fetus. The tree is like a placenta, the stem is like an umbilical cord. Eve's excuse was, "The serpent beguiled me." That the serpent may represent the temptation of sexual passion one might guess from Cyrano de Bergerac's account of God's punishment for the snake. He placed it in Adam's body, where it formed his entrails.[14] Its head nevertheless protruded at the base of his belly, always ready to bite a woman and make her swell with its poison for nine months. Put it all together, and we have the ecological problem: play now, pay later.

2. If aborting is a sin (old archery term that means "missing the mark"), what is redemption or salvation? What *is* the mark?

3. Can abortion be talked about without a framework that explores such phenomena as cruelty to children, infanticide, euthanasia, birth control, suicide, murder, abandonment, war, assassination, self-defense, crowding, sacrifice, self-punishment, hatred, rage, etc.?

4. What if the rules for what's right and what's wrong are a function of time? What if what was sin originally, from a species survival point of view, now, at the present point in our psychosocial evolution, is becoming a duty and a virtue? As Ashley Montague argues, when our ancestors fought to survive, populations were highly selected for their ability to love their children, who had to be greatly valued. Mortality rates were high and births happened at long intervals (approximately four years apart, due to intensive nursing for four to seven years). The process of natural selection placed a high premium on mothers (and others) ministering to children for many years. The same process of natural selection now pressures us to transcend matter and quantity by mind and quality. If we are to survive, we may have to conceptualize the host of future populations wanting to invade our world, pressing to be born through us, as our number one enemy. Sin, then, would be to allow one of *them* to slip into this world. Birth control, abortion, infanticide may have to become our sacred duty.

Abraham's God may soon speak to all of us, asking us to sacrifice our children to prove our faith in a viable future for our species. We need new myths to guide us.

5. Lloyd deMause,[15] a psychohistorian, has amassed evidence to support the view that a change in infant care, if widespread, changes the national character and the course of history in 20-25 years. He claims that the American Revolution would not have been fought had the mothers of those who fought it not abandoned the practice of swaddling.

I truly wonder what sort of revolution we are preparing for now as we are changing our attitudes to pre-and peri-natal care! I want to hazard one prediction only. When child-bearing becomes a genuine choice for women, and those who choose to become mothers can count on a reliable support system, and when delivery practice becomes gentle and humane, and when infants will not be separated from their mothers but will be allowed to bond and tune and heal each other—*then* we can look forward to a life without violence and the realization of our full humanity.

Notes

1. *Encyclopaedia Britannica*, 15th ed., 1978. Propaedia, p. 206.

2. Huxley, Julian, ed. *The Humanist Frame*. London: Allen & Unwin, 1961, p. 431.

3. Maven, A. The Mystic Union: "A Suggested Biological Interpretation." *Jour. Trans Personal Psy.* 1, No. 1 (1969), 51-55.

4. Mott, Francis J. *The Nature of the Self*. London: Allan Wingate, 1959.

5. Rank, Otto. *The Trauma of Birth*. N.Y.: Harper & Row, 1973.

6. Fodor, Nandor. *The Search for the Beloved*. N.Y.: Hermitage, 1949.

7. Laing, R. D. *The Facts of Life*. N.Y.: Pantheon, 1976.

8. Grof, Stanislav. *Realms of the Human Unconscious*. N.Y.: Viking, 1975.

9. Leboyer, Frederick. *Birth without Violence*. N.Y.: Knopf, 1975.

10. Rich, Adrienne. *Of Woman Born*. N.Y.: Norton, 1976.

11. Gordon, M. "The Predicament." *The N.Y. Review of Books*. July 20, 1978, p. 37.

12. Szasz, T. "Nobody Should Decide Who Goes to The Mental Hospital." *The CoEvolution Quarterly*. Summer 1978, pp. 56-69.

13. Bakan, David. *Slaughter of the Innocents*. Toronto: CBC, 1971.

14. Huxley, Francis. *The Way of the Sacred*. London: Aldus, 1974.

15. de Mause, Lloyd. *The History of Childhood*. N.Y.: Psychohistory Press, 1974.

Infant Abortion and Child Abuse: Cause and Effect

Philip G. Ney, M.D.

Thesis and Antithesis

It is argued that unwanted children are abused; therefore, people should have only wanted children.[1][2] Unwanted children not only may be aborted, but should be aborted. They should be aborted now in case they are battered later.[3][4]

It is the child's right to be wanted; ergo, if he is unwanted, it is his right not to be.[5] The aborters will grant this right.

To some there is an apparent association between abortion and child abuse. Therefore, it is argued, to prevent child abuse there should be abortion on request.[6] But there is no convincing evidence that restricted abortion resulted in frequent child abuse. There is no convincing evidence that liberalized abortion has reduced the rate of child abuse; in fact the evidence indicates the opposite:

1. In spite of the fact that abortion on demand has greatly increased in North America, there has been an increase in child battering, e.g., the New York Central Registry reported 22,683 battered children in 1974 and 26,536 in 1975.[7] With this 18-20 percent increase per annum, it is estimated in the next decade there will be 1.5 million battered children, resulting in 50,000 deaths and 300,000 permanently injured children in the United States.[7] The most common cause of death in American children 6-12 months of age is being killed by their own parents.[8]

2. Over 90 percent of the battered children are wanted pregnancies.[9]

3. Abortion was not considered any more frequently among child battering parents than by the controls.[10]

4. Abuse is not more common among defective or retarded children.[11]

5. Adopted children are more frequently abused.[8]

Psychopathogenesis Linking Abortion and Battering

There is evidence and reason to suggest that abortion, rather than preventing child abuse, is the cause of the increase in battered and murdered children. The following mechanisms can be detected:

1. Abortion decreases an individual's instinctual restraint against the occasional rage felt toward those dependent on his or her care.

2. Permissive abortion diminshes the social taboo against aggressing the defenseless.

3. Abortion increases the hostility between the generations.

4. Abortion has devalued children, thus diminishing the value of caring for children.

5. Abortion increases guilt and self-hatred, which the parent takes out on the child.

6. Abortion increases hostile frustration, intensifying the battle of the sexes, for which children are the scapegoat.

7. Abortion truncates the developing mother-infant bond, thereby diminishing her future mothering capability.

I. Diminished Restraint Against Rage

Too often, those of us who treat disturbed children hear parents state, "If she keeps it up, I'll wring her bloody neck" or "Johnny, you're going to push me too far." Not only are these statements becoming more frequent, they are becoming more vehement. Some parents become so frightened of their own rage that they withdraw from involvement with their children or leave home. Others enact that destructive rage, which may injure, maim or kill their children.

In all creatures, a signal of helpless distress from the young will invite either parental care or aggression. The submissive baring of the neck will suddenly stop the dominant wolf's attack on a rival. On the other hand, a healthy seagull tied by one leg, flapping helplessly on the ground, invites the aggressive attack of the whole flock. There is a fine balance between caring and destruction.[12] A cat under normal circumstances, following the birth of her young, will eat the placenta and begin licking her young. If disturbed, however, she will not only eat the placenta, but devour her young.

Whimpering, even across species, produces a tension in people, which is only relieved when the need is attended to or when the whimpering is forcibly, sometimes permanently, stopped. A woman, to abort her helpless young, has to overcome her instinctual impulse to attend to the little one's helplessness. Even though aborters are frequently told, "It's only a piece of tissue," no one can help seeing pictures of fetuses which are visibly human from early life. Even the seasoned aborter, seeing her limp fetus, experiences a profound psychological shock that can produce a serious illness.[13][14] Disgusted nurses find it hard to adjust.[15][16]

The fine nurture-attack balance weighs in favor of aggression when instinctual restraint is weakened by earlier rage against helpless young. The aborting person must suppress the species-preserving instinct. Having done so once, it's easier the next time. The suppressed response is less effective, even when the helplessness is that of a whimpering child. Therefore, more people are responding to the cries of distress with rage or neglect, rather than protection,[17] especially those beaten or neglected themselves when young.[18]

II. Diminished Taboo Against Aggressing Defenseless Young

From ancient times, when an infant's own parent wouldn't nurture or protect him, the neighbors rushed to his aid. If children are unnecessarily beaten, the police, with social sanction, intervene. The same taboo against aggression toward the defenseless is acknowledged in war and, when transgressed by the killing of POWs, the wounded, women or children, it is condemned as an atrocity.

There is nothing more helpless than the unborn baby, who desperately struggles to survive, drawing away in pain from the saline injection or struggling to breathe when he is prematurely and forcibly expelled into the world. More than one person has heard the whimpering of the aborted infant in garbage cans of the pathology lab.[18]

All those who know of the infant's struggle and don't respond, do so with considerable conscious effort. In doing so, they break an ancient taboo. The effect of that taboo in them is weakened with every decision not to act when provoked by the sight and sound of a defenseless, voiceless infant, struggling for survival.

Everyone involved becomes more inclined to passivity in a situation where a battered child screams for help. Every instance of inactivity is reinforced by a gradually diminishing tension, as the person walks away. People used to die in defense of the tribe's young. Now they applaud or stand by helplessly. Helplessness becomes a generalized reaction to the battering of children and influences people much more than they care to admit.

The Increased Hostility Between Generations

"The younger generation has no respect. There ought to be a law to stop those little buggers."

"Damn it, if no one else will, I will."

While adults become increasingly threatened by the demanding younger generation, children become increasingly cynical of their parents.

"They don't give a damn about us, why should we care what happens to them?"

"My old man doesn't give a shit, except for his golf and his girlfriend."

"My old lady didn't want to miss her trip to France, so she had the baby aborted. She probably didn't want me either."

Aborting women felt that they were carrying out "the unconscious wishes of their rejecting mothers, who had not wanted their own birth and had, in many cases, actively tried to prevent it."[19]

With the increasing cynicism, children are less confident of care and thus become increasingly demanding. "Come on old man, give it up, you can't take it with you." Their increasingly demanding behavior threatens the adult, who views with increasing alarm "those little buggers" who might infringe on his rights to enjoyment, or his right to become "myself." The adults, feeling irritated and threatened, feel justified in their attempts to silence the child's demanding behavior.[20]

"You would have done the same thing if your kid kept bugging you all day."

It is abortion which convinces the children that adults probably don't want them and don't care. Because they cannot assume they will be cared for, they become more demanding. These demands threaten adults, who respond with aggression, physical battering being only one form of it.[21]

III. Diminishing Value of Children

With the increasing number of abortions by choice, there should be an increased number of women who really wanted their children. On the contrary, there appears to be an increased number of people who would rather not have kids. To Ann Landers' question in her newspaper column, 70 percent of 10,000 couples indicated they would rather not have had children. There has been a recent, abrupt shift toward zero or negative population growth. The proportion of freshmen college women wanting two or fewer children in 1970 was 50 percent, and in 1973 it was 64 percent.[22]

If the new model car is scrapped when it's only part way along the assembly line, it is apparent to all buyers that the car must be defective and probably not worth much. Abortion diminishes the value of all people, particularly children. When the destruction of the unborn child is socially sanctioned and even applauded, the child can't have much value. More than anyone, children realize they are becoming worth less. Thus, the rate of suicide has increased correspondingly.

If society adheres to the ethic that the unborn child only has value when he is wanted,[1][5] that ethic can easily be applied to small children. Logically, when people stop wanting a child, he has lost value. If the unborn has no value and it is all right to kill him, then it is defensible to kill children who have lost value because they are now unwanted.

People do not harm what they highly value. As children decline in value, it becomes easier to neglect and dispose of them. Besides, both those who abort children[23] and those who murder them[24] say they do it "out of love."

IV. Abortion Results in Two Kinds of Guilt
Guilt in the aborting mother.

Severe guilt is found in 2 to 23 percent, depending upon the type of study.[25] These rates were found on surveys and questionnaires, but more detailed interviews find "without exception, there are feelings of guilt or profound regret." "All the women felt that they had lost an important part of themselves." "They had a feeling that they had been symbolically killing themselves."[19] Guilt is one of the major factors causing battering and infanticide. There are "intolerable feelings of self-hatred, which the parent takes out on the child."[26] Abortion results in guilt, and guilt contributes to child battering.

In both battering parents and women who abort, there is a significant lack of self-esteem.[27][28][29] It appears that women who place no value on their finest creation do so because they have poor self-esteem. However, the abortion contributes to that lowered self-esteem, which contributes to child battering. Battering also results in increased guilt, which could lead to more frequent abortions of subsequent pregnancies.

Both abortion and child battering[30][31] contain the element of denial of one's own aggressiveness and a projection onto the child, who is seen as the aggressor and dealt with accordingly.
The survivor syndrome.

Those children who are not aborted in a family where an abortion was done experience the "survivor syndrome," a mixture of guilt and anger.[32] Guilt produces depression, which shows as irritability and lethargy, which to the parents smacks of rudeness and disrespect, the very things that trigger many batterings.[33]

The guilt-ridden survivor children also feel an anger toward their parents, but this is displaced onto smaller siblings. The fighting between children sparks an anger in the parents, which precipitates battering. In some instances, the child triggers the parental aggression because he feels that, as a result of his own aggressive feelings, he should be punished. "You killed my baby brother, go ahead and kill me."

When these children grow up, their guilt could contribute to an increase in rates of abortion and battering.

Battle of the Sexes

For all the good things that "women's liberation" has accomplished, one untoward effect is that men are increasingly threatened by women. Women, on the other hand, become increasingly bitter toward men, particularly those who, having impregnated them, pressure them into having an abortion.[34][35]

Marital stress occurs in 67 percent of battered baby cases and interparental violence in 37 percent.[36] The battered baby syndrome seems to go with a battered wife syndrome.

The increasing hostility of men toward women in part stems from their growing awareness that they have a declining influence in the production of children:

a. Men no longer have a legal right to participate in the decision regarding the abortion of their baby.[37][38]

b. There is an increased proportion of male babies being aborted on the basis of sex.

c. Few men have success in custody battles for their children.[39][40]

d. With the establishment of sperm banks and the increasing possibility of test-tube babies, men deem themselves and are so deemed by some groups, e.g., Daughters of Lilith, as unnecessary.

In an increasingly sedentary society, to which many men cannot adapt, men more than women have stress diseases and have a life expectancy 6 to 8 years less. Finding that they cannot compete and that women are better in debate, some men, unable to express their pent-up rage, take out their displaced aggression on children. On the other hand, frequently women who name their illegitimate child after the departed boyfriend, displace their aggression onto that child.

Some men, feeling that size is their only remaining weapon when verbally cornered, beat their wives, who then beat the child.[10] Others, in frustration, leave home, another prominent antecedent to child battering.[10]

The Breakdown in the Ability to Mother

Increasing evidence indicates that "any phenomenon which may intervene in the early attachment of the mother to child may be an important contributor to the pathogenesis of child abuse."[11] The establishment of the mother-infant bond is a delicate business and can be easily influenced by subtle changes in mother or infant.

Poor bonding between mother and infant may be due to a number of factors:

1. Abnormalities in the child, low birth weight, retardation, poor skin condition, or anything which makes the mother less affectionate toward her infant.[41][42]

2. An immediate post-partum separation because of an illness in the mother.[43]

3. Post-partum depression as a result of a previous loss.

One-third of the mothers with children diagnosed as having failed to thrive were mourning the loss of a close relative. It has been found that if one twin dies, the mother has difficulty attaching to the survivor.[44] Any stress—the death of a close friend, a previous abortion, or loss of previous children—may delay preparation for the infant and retard bond formation.[45] Longer and more intense mourning was seen in mothers for whom pregnancy was a positive experience. The mothers grieved whether an infant lived one hour or twelve days, whether he weighed 3,000 grams or a nonviable 580 grams, and whether the pregnancy was planned or unplanned.[44]

Ambivalence during the pregnancy regarding the mother's wanting or not wanting the child does not seem to have an effect on bond formation. In fact, the shakeup in pregnancy, sometimes seen as an alarm reaction for mothers, is a readying of the circuits preparing her for new attachments.[46]

The first few hours of mother-infant contact are crucial to the establishment of that bond which sustains the infant. DeChateau's[47] beautiful research project was able to demonstrate that an extra fifteen to twenty minutes of sucking and skin contact during the first hour post-delivery had such a marked impact on children, as compared with matched controls, that there was a measurable effect three months later. At that time, subjects having had extra contact smiled more and cried less. Their mothers were also different. They spent more time kissing their children, looking at them, and breast-feeding them. Those given extra time with skin contact or breast-feeding had babies that gained weight faster, had fewer infections, and had higher I.Q.s.[44]

Bonding develops throughout pregnancy and becomes set when the infant is born. Many women start off with a strong ambivalence toward having a child, but gradually come to terms with the knowledge that they are mothers. Initially, women identify a growing baby as an integral part of themselves. With quickening,

the baby becomes established as a separate individual, often pro-
voking elaborate fantasies. Throughout this, unplanned pregnancies gradually become more accepted.[48]

In rats, hormones determine nesting behavior. The further
along in the pregnancy that the mother is delivered by Caesarian
section, the more maternal behavior she shows.[49] Virgin rats cross-
transfused from pregnant rats respond to the increasing levels of
estradiol and engage in elaborate maternal behavior.[50]

There are similar large changes in the hormonal levels of
women, and they produce a similar maternal mind-set.[51][52] It appears the hormones create an attitude of determined protection
and self-sacrificing nurturing. The hormonal changes in mothers
throughout the ages must have been sufficiently powerful to overcome the resistances to pregnancy, even during times of war, famine, and pestilence.

More motherly and more mature women feel more post-abortion guilt.[53] Post-partum primiparas generally show less anxiety,
fearfulness and hostilities than do multiparas, although one would
expect quite the opposite. It appears that the bonding to the infant
not only increases throughout the pregnancy, but the outcome of
one pregnancy influences the bonding of the next.[54] Therefore, if
the pregnancy does not culminate in a live child, the same responses will not develop as well in subsequent pregnancies.

Mothers report that abortion is a vicarious suicide.[19] In the
early stages of pregnancy, when the infant is perceived as an extension of the mother's self, by aborting she not only destroys a
part of herself, she interrupts a developing bond. In later stages of
pregnancy, when the mother is aware of killing a separate entity,
she breaks the bond that has developed between her and a baby.
The baby was a reality in the mother's mind and, when aborted, in
some women became a phantom child with whom she talked.[55]

Thus, it would appear that those who abort their infants at any
stage of pregnancy interrupt a very delicate mechanism and sever
the developing bond that is critical for the infant's protection
against the mother's carelessness or rage. It is hypothesized that,
once bonding is interrupted in the primipara, there are long-lasting psychological changes which make it more difficult for the
same bond to develop in subsequent pregnancies. For this reason,
it is likely that abortion contributes to bonding failure, an important cause of child battering. Consequently, as rates of abortion increase, rates of battering will increase proportionately.

Case History

Mercy, a four-year-old child, was hospitalized with dehydration and malnourishment so severe she almost died. The depressed, despondent mother agreed that the child had been neglected, but reasoned it was because the child had been so quiet and placid. Interviewing the mother, it was obvious she had little affection for the child, was unobservant of the child's needs, trembled when she picked her up, and held her stiffly. At the same time, the mother was adamant that the child was hers and resisted the idea of foster home placement.

The social worker argued, with the support of a pediatrician, that the child had been unwanted and therefore would continue to be neglected. In fact, the child should have been aborted. A more detailed history uncovered the fact that the mother, pregnant at the age of seventeen, was coerced by parents and boyfriend into marriage. Yet she enjoyed her first child and looked after it very well. When she became pregnant two months after the birth of her first, her husband (who later left her) continually pressured her into having an abortion. Eventually, she reluctantly agreed, partly on the grounds, submitted by the physician, that she had had measles. Following the abortion, she felt very guilty, and resentful of those who had persuaded her against her wishes. She often ruminated on whether the child was indeed deformed, but never had the courage to ask her doctor. During her third pregnancy, she was happy. When the baby was born, her husband forbade her to breast-feed because it would embarrass him. The mother gradually began neglecting the child and the father left home.

At first inquiry, it appeared that the mother was about to have another unwanted child, which she would neglect. A better explanation was that the neglect resulted from the mother's depression subsequent to the abortion of her second pregnancy. Guilt and tension surrounding the birth of Mercy further interrupted the formation of the mother-infant bond, so that the mother felt no tension and did not respond to the child's increasingly feeble cries. In fact, the mother went dancing.

Summary

The argument that unwanted children will be abused and therefore should be aborted is no new argument. It was used throughout the centuries in any instance where the unwanted or undesirables were felt to be infringing on the rights or pleasures of those in power.[56] The "angel-makers" used it to justify killing babies.[1] Plantation owners used it to justify slavery. The Nazis used it

to justify genocide.[57] Abortion appears to be in the tradition of violent pseudo-solutions, which only compound complex personal
and social problems.

Abortion not only increases the rates of child battering at
present, it will increase the tendency to batter and abort in suc-
ceeding generations. Abortion, producing guilt both in the mother
and in the children who survive, increases the probability of displaced hostility, which results in so many battered, murdered children. More importantly, by interrupting the formation of the delicate mechanism which promotes mother-infant bonding, it puts at
risk millions of babies who are not aborted.

Humanity has become an endangered species. Evidence indicates that, once implemented, abortion changes attitudes toward
infants, such that birth rates do not increase, even when the abortion law is tightened.[25] Although overpopulation has been touted
as the most critical problem in the world, underpopulation in
Western countries has become perhaps the most burning issue in
recorded history. A rapid decline in population is something that
Western countries cannot deal with. There is no mechanism for
enabling the major institutions and the economy to adjust.

When we are so careful not to tamper with the delicate bal-
ances of plant and animal ecology, one wonders why we are so ignorant of the effects that killing the unborn infants of the human
species is having on all humanity. There is no question that the
species-specific, instinctual behavior of humans has safeguarded
the young. It has made survival possible through millenia of anni-
hilating disasters. What war, famine, and pestilence could not ac-
complish, medicine in the name of liberated humanism is now
performing. We have disrupted a very delicate balance, turning
parents against their own offspring. There may be no turning back.

References

1. Beck, M. B. "The Destiny of the Unwanted Child." *Abortion
   and the Unwanted Child.* ed. Reiterman, C. New York: Springer, 1971.

2. Dennis, Magda. *In Necessity and Sorrow, Life and Death in an
   Abortion Hospital.* New York: Basic Books, 1976.

3. Calef, V. "The Hostility of Parents of Children: Some Notes on
   Fertility, Child Abuse, and Abortion." *Int. J. Psychoanal. Psychother.* 1: 79-96, 1972.

4. Caffey, J. "The Parent-Infant Traumatic Stress Syndrome." *Am. J. Roentgn. Rad. Ther. Nucl. Med.* 114: 218-229, 1972.

5. Hardin, G. "Abortion for the Children's Sake." *Abortion and the Unwanted Child.* ed. Reiterman, C. New York: Springer, 1971.

6. Kempe, C. H., and Helfer, R. E. *Helping the Battered Child and His Family.* Philadelphia and Toronto: R. B. Lippincott, 1972.

7. Fontana, V. J., and Bersharov, D. J. *The Maltreated Child.* Springfield: Charles C. Thomas, 1977.

8. Schmitt, B. D., and Kempre, C. H. *Child Abuse: Management and Prevention of the Battered Child Syndrome.* Basle: Ciba-Geigy, 1975.

9. Lenoski, E. F. "Translating Injury Data into Preventive Health Care Services. Physical Child Abuse." Dept. of Pediatrics, University of Southern California, unpublished, 1976.

10. Smith, S. M. *The Battered Child Syndrome.* London: Butterworth's, 1975.

11. Martin, H. P., ed. *The Abused Child.* Cambridge: Ballinger Publishing Company, 1976.

12. Brody, Sylvia. *Patterns of Mothering.* New York: International University Press, 1956.

13. Brew, C. "Induced Abortion After Feeling Fetal Movements: Causes and Emotional Consequences." *J. Bio. Soc. Sci.* 10: 203-208, 1978.

14. Lipper, S., et al. "Obsessive-Compulsive Neurosis After Viewing the Fetus During Therapeutic Abortion." *Am. J. Psychother.* 30: 666-674, 1976.

15. McDermott, J. F., and Char, W. F. "Abortion Repeal in Hawaii: An Unexpected Crisis in Patient Care." *Am. J. Orthopsychiat.* 41: 620-629, 1971.

16. Kane, F. J. et al. "Emotional Reactions in Abortion Services Personnel." *Arch. Gen. Psychiat.* 28: 409-412, 1973.

17. Hunter, R. S. et al. "Antecedents of Child Abuse and Neglect in Premature Infants." *Pediatrics.* 61: 629-635, 1978.

18. Merry, D. C. "Winnipeg General Hospital Pathologist Finds Baby Boy Whimpering in a Garbage Bag by the Hospital Incinerator." *Victoria Daily Colonist.* April 5, 1972.

19. Kent, I. et al. "Emotional Sequelae to Elective Abortion." *B. C. Med. J.* 20: 118-119, 1978.

20. Margrain, S. A. "Review: Battered Children, Their Parents,

Treatment, and Prevention." *Child Care Health Dev.* 3: 463-499, 1977.

21. Baer, A. M. et al. "Covert Forms of Child Abuse: A Preliminary Study." *Child Psychiat. Hum. Dev.* 8: 115-128, 1977.

22. Wilson, K. M. "Today's Women Students: New Outlooks, Options." *Educational Testing Service.* 1: 5-8, 1974.

23. Gardner, R. *Abortion, A Personal Dilemma.* Grand Rapids: M. B. Erdmans Publishing Co., 1972.

24. Resnick, P. J. "Child Murder by Parents: A Psychiatric Review of Filicide." *Am. J. Psychiat.* 126: 325-328, 1969.

25. Moore-Caver, E. C. "The International Inventory on Information on Induced Abortion." International Institute for the Study of Human Reproduction, Columbia University, 1974.

26. Galdston, R. "Proceedings of Conference on Patterns of Parental Behavior Leading to Physical Abuse of Children." University of Colorado School of Medicine, unpublished, 1966.

27. Merrill, E. J. "Physical Abuse of Children, An Agency Study." *Protecting the Battered Child.* ed., V. DeFrancis. Denver: Children's Division, American Humane Association, 1962.

28. Galdston, R. "Observations on Children Who Have Been Physically Abused and Their Parents." *Am. J. Psychiat.* 122: 440-443, 1965.

29. Hutcherson, J. R. "The Self-Concept of Women at the Time of Elective Abortion." *Dissertation Abstracts International.* 33: (11-b), 5493, May 1973.

30. Smoller, B. et al. "A Psychological Theory of Child Abuse." *Psychiat. Q.* 49: 38-44, 1977.

31. Burkle, F. M. "A Developmental Approach to Post-Partum Abortion Depression." *Practitioner.* 218: 217-225, 1977.

32. Gyomroi, E. L. "The Analysis of a Young Concentration Camp Victim." *Psychoanalytic Study of the Child.* 18: 484-498, 1963.

33. Ryan, M. G. et al. "One Hundred and Eighty-Seven Cases of Child Abuse and Neglect." *Med. J. Aust.* 2: 623-628, 1972.

34. Blake, J. T. "Abortion and Public Opinion: The 1960-1970 Decade." *Science.* 171: 540-549, February 12, 1971.

35. White, R. B. "Induced Abortion: A Survey of Their Psychiatric Implications, Complications, and Indications." *Texas Reports in Biology and Medicine.* 24: 531-535, 1966.

36. Sills, J. A. et al. "Non-Accidental Injury: A Two-Year Study in Central Liverpool." *Dev. Med. Child Neurol.* 19: 26-33, 1977.

37. Planned Parenthood. "World Population." Washington Memo, October 27, 1976.

38. *Planned Parenthood of Central Missouri* v. *Danforth*, 428 U.S. 52, 67-73 (1976).

39. Goldstein, J.; Freud, A.; and Solnit, H. A. *Beyond the Best Interests of the Child.* New York: The Free Press, 1970.

40. Deredeyn, A. T. "Child Custody Contests in Historical Perspective." *Am. J. Psychiat.* 133: 1369-1376, 1976.

41. Lynch, M. A. et al. "Predicting Child Abuse: Signs of Bonding Failure in the Maternity Hospital." *Brit. Med. J.* 1: 1624-1626, 1977.

42. Minde, K. et al. "Interactions of Mothers and Nurses with Premature Infants." *Can. Med. Assoc. J.* 113: 741-746, 1975.

43. tenBensel, R. W., and Paxson, C. L. "Child Abuse Following Early Post-Partum Separation." *J. Pediatr.* 90: 490-494, 1977.

44. Klaus, M. H., and Kennell, J. H. *Maternal-Infant Bonding.* St. Louis: C. U. Mosby Co., 1976.

45. Colman, A. D., and Colman, L. L. *Pregnancy: The Psychological Experience.* New York: Herder and Herder, 1971.

46. Brazelton, T. B. "Effect of Maternal Expectations on Early Infant Behavior." *Early Child Development Care.* 2: 259-273, 1973.

47. DeChateau, P. et al. "Long-Term Effects of Mother-Infant Behavior of Extra Contact During the First Hour Post-Partum. *Acta. Psychiat. Scand.* 66: 145-151, 1977.

48. Brazelton, T. B., et al. "Parent-Infant Interaction." CIBA Foundation Symposium Amsterdam: Elsevier Publishing Co., 1975.

49. Rosenblat, J. S., and Segal, H. I. "Hysterectomy-Induced Maternal Behavior During Pregnancy in Rats." *J. Comp. Physiol. Psychol.* 89: 685-700, 197 .

50. Torkel, J., and Rosenblat, J. S. "Hormonal Factors Underlying Maternal Behavior at Parturition: Cross-Transfusion Between the Freely Moving Rats." *J. Comp. Physiol. Psychol.* 80: 365-371, 1972.

51. Turnbull, A. C., et al. "Significant Fall in Progesterone and Rise in Estradiol in Human Peripheral Placenta Before Onset of Labor." *Lancet.* 1: 101-103, 1974.

52. Dewhurst, C. J., ed. *Integrated Obstetrics and Gynecology for Post-Graduates.* Oxford: Blackwell Scientific Publications, 1972.

53. Pare, C. B., and Hermione, R. "Follow-up of Patients Referred for Termination of Pregnancy." *Lancet.* 1: 635-637, 1970.

54. Wright, B. "Parental Attachment to Premature and Seriously Ill Infants." Unpublished Master's thesis, Michigan State University, 1977.

55. Liebman, M. H., and Zimmer, J. S. "Abortion Sequelae: Fact and Fallacy." Paper presented at the symposium, Psychological Aspects of Abortion, Loyola University, Chicago, 1978.

56. Sanford, N., et al. *Sanctions for Evil.* San Francisco: Deacon Press, 1971.

57. Brown, H. O. J. "The German Court's Decision: A Translation of the Summary." *Human Life Review,* Summer, 1975 pp. 75-5.

Abortion—Pain or Pleasure?

Howard W. Fisher, M.D.

Introduction

Review of the literature might lead one to conclude that abortion is safe medically and emotionally.[1]

In 1975, three out of ten pregnancies ended in abortion; six out of ten in New York. Washington, D.C. saw twice the number of abortions as live-born children.[2] One in three abortions done in the U.S. in 1975 were on teenage girls.[3] Forty percent of women conceive again within three years of an abortion.[4]

Abortion is said to be more acceptable in better-educated women,[5] unless actual pictures of the procedure are shown them.[6]

This study seeks to understand abortion as one kind of behavior, contrasting it with other behaviors seen in a sample of 24 women electing induced abortion as an alternative between 1971 and 1978. It is a retrospective study with data drawn from every patient with a history of induced abortion evaluated by a private psychiatrist during those years. None of these women had been seen because of abortion-related symptoms. It is a preliminary, tentative, exploratory attempt to see if women electing abortion differ in discernible ways from other women.

As a control group, 13 women sustaining spontaneous miscarriages were randomly selected from among the records during those years and compared with the study sample.

Sampling

Control Group

Records of 13 women with a history of spontaneous miscarriage of one or more pregnancies were chosen at random from files containing evaluations done by the author between 1971 and 1978. One of these women also had an induced abortion.

There were five women who miscarried once, two women who miscarried twice and six women who lost three or more pregnancies, some of them consecutively.

Study Group

Records of 24 women with a history of induced abortion were studied. These represented every case referred between 1971 and 1978. Of these, six women had been illegally aborted, under non-hospital conditions. (This data will be found in parentheses beside study.) The rest were deemed legitimate, legal abortions done for presumed medical indication in hospitals thought to be reputable by presumably licensed physician gynecologists. Also studied was a woman who had threatened abortion but who had changed her mind. The data is as follows:

Race	Study	Controls
White	21 (6)	9
Black	2	2
Indian	1	1
Mexican	0	1

Age	Study	Controls	Religion	Study	Controls
15-20	6 (2)	0	Catholic	3 (1)	3
21-26	6	2	Protestant	6 (1)	6
27-32	8	4	Jewish	2 (2)	0
33-38	1 (1)	3	Baptist	2 (2)	1
39-44	1 (1)	1	None	2	0
45-50	0	2	Unknown	9	3
51-55	2 (2)	1			

Referral Source	Study	Controls
Gynecologist	8	2
Self	4 (1)	0
General Practitioner	2	3
Disability (SSA)	1 (1)	2
Mother	2	0
Emergency Room	1	0
Medical Exchange	1 (1)	0
Another Patient	1	1
Chemical Dependency Counselor	0	1
Chemical Dependency Unit	0	1
Employer	1	0
Probation Officer	1 (1)	0
Another Psychiatrist	0	1
Unknown	2 (2)	2

Marital Status	Study	Controls	Comment on Study Group
Single	5 (1)	0	Woman who had 7 abortions cannot marry because of them
Divorced			
Once	9 (2)	2	3 men deserted around time of pregnancy
Twice	1	1	One husband alcoholic
Thrice	1 (1)	0	One husband alcoholic
Separated			
From 1st husband	5 (1)	1	One husband alcoholic
From 2nd husband	1	1	All husbands alcoholic
From 3rd husband	0	1	
Married			
Once	2 (1)	4	One marriage "unhappy"
Twice	0	2	
Widowed	0	1	Twice married

Medical History

General Medical	Study	Controls
Obesity as a child	2 (1)	1
as an adult	4 (1)	1
Chronic pulmonary disease	2 (1)	4
Pneumonia	1	1
Ulcer	3	1
Pancreatitis	1	1

Post-Surgical

	Study	Controls
Cholecystectomy	0	1
Splenectomy (traumatic)	0	1
Multiple	0	1

Non-Specific

	Study	Controls
Use of marijuana alone	1 (1)	0
Lesbianism	1 (1)	0

Gynecological

	Study	Controls
PID (Chronic)	6 (1)	2
Non-orgasmic	5 (1)	1
Ligation after abortion	4 (2)	0
Ligation not after abortion	1	2
Infertility	3 (1)	2
Hysterectomy	2	1
Hysterectomy and Bilat S&O	2	0
Dyspareunia	1	0
Conflict over Dalkon Shield	1	0
Cancer of the cervix	1	0
Infant prematurity	0	1
Tubal pregnancy	0	1
C-Section	1	0
Attempted self-induced abortion	1	0
Pelvic pain	0	1

Neurological

	Study	Controls
Seizures	0	1

Psychiatric Diagnoses

(As defined by the Diagnostic and Statistical Manual of the American Psychiatric Association, 1968)

Eleven of the study women and four of the controls had been hospitalized under the care of the author. Nine of the study group and one of the controls had undergone psychological testing, including an MMPI, WAIS, Rorschach, and Bender Gestalt. One of the illegal aborters had been hospitalized and she had psychologicals. One of the illegal aborters had undergone outpatient psychologicals.

	Study	Controls
Character Disorder		
Chemical Dependency	20 (2)	7
Not abusing chemicals	5	5
Depression (denied)	2	0
Psychosis at some time	15 (2)	2*
Neurotic symptoms at some time		
Phobic	7 (1)	0
Conversion	5	1**
Dissociative	1 (1)	0
Hypochondriacal	1 (1)	3
Mental Retardation	1	0
Other additional features		
Wrist cutting	1 (1)	0
Overdosing	2 (2)	0

*after miscarriage
**compensation

Psychiatric Treatment

Of those getting psychiatric care, the women were the only ones doing so (that is, their significant others were not getting help) and only three did, one after childbirth. Ten of the study group continued in treatment with the author. One of the controls followed through.

Past Psychiatric Care	Study	Controls
Hospitalization	6	2*
Office care	3 (1)	0
Symptoms not treated		
"Ill all my life"	1	1
Chronic depression	1	0
Frequenting emergency rooms	1	0
Rejection by the army	1	1
Conversion paralysis	1	0
Hypochondriasis (frequent hospitalizations)	0	2
Hyperventilation	0	1

*after miscarriage

History of Relationships	Study	Controls
Father abandoned	3	0
Mother abandoned	4	0
Parents divorced	3	0
Parents never married	2	0
Father had no contact	1	0
Chemical dependency		
Father	7	1
Mother	0	0
Husband	10	1
Boyfriend	6 (1)	0
Violence		
Assault on patient	10 (3)	3
Assault by patient	4 (1)	0

Education	Study	Controls
Incomplete High School	12 (2)	4
High School Diploma	7 (2)	4
Incomplete College	4 (2)	1
Degree from College	1	0
Unknown	0	4

Employment History	Study	Controls
Unskilled Work	8 (3)	6
None	1 (1)	1
Many jobs	1	1
Student	2	0
Aid to Disabled	1 (1)	0
Skilled Work	5 (1)	1
Homemaker	1 (1)	0
Prostitute	2	0
Unknown	3	4

Debt History	Study	Controls
County Assistance	15 (3)	4
Bankrupt	1	1
Fired	1	0

Arrests	Study	Controls
Forgery	4 (2)	1
Assault (on a stranger)	2	0
Theft	2 (1)	0
Fraud	1	0
Prostitution	1	0
Incorrigibility	1 (1)	0
Unknown charge	0	1

Data on Induced Abortion

All but two women had had one abortion. One woman had had three abortions. One woman had had seven abortions. The latter two cases had both completed psychologicals. Seven women had undergone abortion within a year of the consultation. The longest period since the abortion was 22 years.

The woman having three abortions had sustained a postpartum schizophrenic reaction bringing her to psychiatric care. She was finally ligated.

The woman having seven abortions had been abandoned by her father when she was three and later seduced by her brother. She told her psychiatrist that she had hoped her lover would have tried to stop her during each of the seven abortions. Following psychiatric care by the author, she had a child and gave it up for adoption, returning to inform the author on one occasion. She reported profound ambivalence about giving up the child.

There was the case of a woman who threatened abortion but did not carry it out. She was a 24-year-old single alcoholic Indian prostitute on medical assistance who had one year of general college. She had already placed one child, after having had two living children by two different men. She had been phobic. Medical history included gonorrhea and a period in jail. She was referred for psychiatric evaluation by another patient. Her decision *not* to abort followed the loss of her suitor who left after she made the threat.

Data on Induced Abortion

Who Sought?	Number
Unknown	19
Psychiatrist	0
Father	1
Mother	1
Patient	1
Mother and Boyfriend	1
Social worker and Boyfriend	1

How Surfaced as Important	Number
Hospitalized for psychosis	1
for depression	1
Depressed (not hospitalized)	
over the abortion	1
over husband leaving	1
phobic neurosis	1
husband confessed not his child	1

The control group had a total of four out-of-wedlock children, one by ex-husband and a total of two children placed for adoption.

Psychological Dynamics

The following data represents accumulated dynamics using clinical interview and psychological testing.

This sample is ill medically and psychiatrically, low in achievment, and prone to act out in self-destructive ways. They appear "psychopathic" or "borderline" (as defined by Kernberg[7] and Mas-

Data on Induced Abortions

No. of Children Prior to Abortion	Study	Comment	Controls
One	2	One adopted out	1
Two	3	One crib death	1
Three	2 (1)	Placed due to beatings	0

No. of Children After Abortion	Study	Comment	Controls
One	11	Four kids were out of wedlock, one was given to father	2
Two	4	One out of wedlock, one mulatto child given up after self-induced abortion	0
Three	2	One out of wedlock	2
Four	2	Two placed	1
Six	0		1*

*(slew of miscarriages—not consecutive)

terson[8]). There was a substantial element of underlying depression present in both study and control subjects.

Ambivalence was a cardinal feature in all subjects, seen most clearly in the patient having seven abortions. Also characteristic was use of denial.

Uniformly present in both study and control groups were 1) incomplete separation-individuation from the maternal object producing a primary ambivalence regarding attachment, as found by Mahler[9] and Bowlby.[10] This hostile-dependent relationship found later expression in 2) conflict with authority, both male and female.

Incomplete separation from mother led to a confusion regarding self-object differentiation and resentment of any external object reminding the self of dependency. The resentment took the form of rejection of the female and maternal role which led to confusion regarding sexual identity.[11] This rejection led to low self-esteem. The resentment was projected externally as anger. Anger and resentment produced a need for self-punishment and a need to punish something outside the self, a kind of revenge.

Confusion of sexual identity led to attempts to "prove" femininity, with sexual acting out and resultant pregnancy. This is why contraception "fails." Actually the pregnancy is not totally "unwanted."[12] Anger produced a kind of martyred self-destructive existence in these subjects, with confused games of rejection and sabotage of relationships, with complete absence of conscious awareness. Intelligence or education made the games more complex but not more available to understanding by the person.[6] It is this peculiar inability to profit from experience which has been said to characterize the psychopath.[12] The anger brings with it the complication of drug and/or alcohol abuse to escape the inner pressure.

This anger produces a kind of mistrust of oneself and the world around, blocking effective relationships, making adjustment difficult and psychiatric treatment arduous. Treatment of these character disorders is discussed by Dr. Masterson in his work with borderline adolescents.[8] However, martyrdom is extremely resistant to psychiatric treatment.[13]

Anger at authority has a coexisting defense reflecting infantile omnipotence called *entitlement* which projects responsibility for personal failure to others and demands compensation for grievances. This defense justifies abortion as "deserved" because it is an act of retribution carried out against a threatening object and thus carries with it lessened guilt.

A pregnancy is "outside" the psychological self, but inside the physical self. Not until quickening can some women tell there is a separate life within them. After the baby kicks, it is harder to deny the separation. Psychological birth occurs long after physical birth. As long as the pregnancy is indistinguishable from the inner self, the woman can be "unaware" of it and logically abort "it" as though it was not there. Because of incomplete separation-individuation, these women have difficulty conceiving of the fetus as separate because of problems with self-object discrimination. This is a basic problem in reality testing. In a sense, the fetus is like an inner feeling that is denied, something these women did regularly with all of their feelings, especially angry ones.

Since pregnancy is viewed as a punishment visited on the self, abortion is a "logical" attempt to rid the self of painful responsibility, a form of expiation. But psychologically, abortion is further self-punishment which occurs because the "thing" that is sacrificed is felt to be a portion of the self. It is as though the self seeks the pleasure of conception and the pain of loss in one unconscious moment, making abortion truly masochistic.

There is, however, a sadistic component to this anger, punishing five external objects simultaneously: husband (father-mother substitute), father, mother, relevant siblings, and baby (seen unconsciously as a combination of all of these objects).

Discussion

Pregnancy can be a deterrent to growth, even within marriage. It represents a crisis for both partners.[14] Emotional growth can be seen as the result of willingness to accept restrictions imposed by a totally separate object who is viewed as significant to the needs of the self. This definition applies to spouse and fetus alike.

Poor relationships with men (father figures, authority figures) led to marital problems in the sample. The problem these women face is accepting external restrictions and growing from them or regressing to an infantile hedonism. It is this regression that seems to characterize this sample and defines them as masochistic.

It is interesting that women who need self-punishment do not abort themselves more often. Only one patient in this sample tried that and she was retarded. The projection of responsibility to an external punishing agent (physician) accomplishes a lessening of guilt. Abortion is done "to" the woman, with her as only a passive participant. This is further indication of masochism.

The law of retribution known as the Talion Law—an eye for an eye—has been known for centuries and is operating in every person's unconscious. It is the expression of "fairness" that those who hurt you are to be hurt in return, in like measure. "A child for a child" can now be seen as a new wrinkle on this ancient law: The sacrifice of the emotional self (the child within us) as a result of the hostile scapegoating by a vengeful parent producing a hateful child.

Freud's work on the fantasy "A Child Is Being Beaten"[15] and "A Case of Homosexuality in a Woman"[16] may have peculiar relevance for abortion.

Pregnancy is truly a transitional object[17] for some women, linking the self with the outside world, both for mother and fetus. Birthing means to introduce the conceptus to the world. This responsibility has appropriately been felt as a heavy one by women, despite the fact that it used to bring them great joy. The weight of this responsibility has traditionally fallen on women exclusively, and has perhaps given rise to the Biblical injunction, "In sorrow shalt thou bring forth children," when they realized they could not share this burden with a helpful spouse.

It will remain to be validated by other researchers whether a masochistic lifestyle can be found in other groups of women seeking induced abortion. If this is so, perhaps society ought not offer this alternative for further devaluation of the self, and physicians should not be manipulated[4][18][19] into participating in a procedure which can bring further loss of hope to already troubled patients.

It is interesting to speculate whether abortion is itself a symptom of the manipulation of medicine by antisocial personalities bent on punishing their father-figures along with themselves. If that is so, and that symptom is allowed to become a disease of epidemic proportions, it may spell the demise of the whole of medicine and of society.

Summary

Tentative findings of this study are that abortion can be a symptom of underlying emotional disturbance[20] in the women and of a marital problem.[21] Abortion would seem to be a symbol of failure. There is indication it may be done at the convenience of someone other than the woman. All of these subjects were in chaos. Few of them had compulsive traits. Poor relationships make this sample difficult to treat. The implications of martyrdom are discussed. The question is whether to participate in a destructive process once it is clear it cannot be interrupted. That is, are physicians merely accomplices in self-destructive behavior? This was more easily seen in the case of psychiatrists[19] until the Supreme Court made psychiatric opinion irrelevant.

We need more data on this problem. It is a particularly strange commentary on our times that destruction of others and of self can be denied in so many subtle ways, and expressed in so many subtle ways. It can be no accident that physicians participating in abortion sought to prevent the keeping of records that might contain the data needed to expose these problems.

In the opinion of this author, the only solution to this problem is through encouragement of children's growth and separation-individuation, recognizing them as separate living beings from the moment of conception, and encouraging their relations with the outside world, a process which begins at conception and, it is hoped, continues throughout life.

Bibliography

1. Simon, N. M. et al. "Psychiatric Sequelae of Abortion—Review of the Literature 1935-64." *Arch. Gen. Psychiat.* 15: 378-89, October 1966.

2. U.S. Census Bureau. "Perspectives in American Fertility." 1975.

3. McAnarney, E. "Adolescent Pregnancy—A National Priority." *Am. J. Dis. Child.* 132: 125, February 1978.

4. Kane, F. J., et al. "Therapeutic Abortion—Quo Vadimus." *Psychosom.* IX: 202-7, July-August 1968.

5. Bogen, I. "Attitudes of Women Who Have Had Abortions." *J. of Sexual Research.* 10:2: 97-109, May 1974.

6. Brennan, W. C. "Abortion and the Techniques of Neutralization." *J. of Health and Soc. Behav.* pp. 358-64.

7. Kernberg, O. *Borderline Conditions and Pathological Narcissism.* New York: Jason Aronson, 1975.

8. Masterson, J. F. "Treatment of the Adolescent with Borderline Syndrome: A Problem in Separation-Individuation." *Bull. of the Menning. Clin.* 35: 5-18, 1971.

9. Mahler, M. S., et al. "Certain Aspects of the Separation-Individuation Phase." *Psychoanal. Q.* 32: 1-14, 1963.

10. Bowlby, J. "The Nature of the Child's Tie to his Mother." *Int. J. Psychoanal.* 39: 350, 1958.

11. Deutch, H. *The Psychology of Women.* 11: 179-94, 1945.

12. Johnson, A., et al. "Genesis of Antisocial Acting Out in Chil-

dren and Adults." *Psychoanal. Q.* 21: 323-43, 1952.

13. Riek, T. Chapter on feminine masochism in *Masochism in Sex and Society.* New York: Grove Press, 1962.

14. Hott, J. R. "Crisis of Expectant Fatherhood." *Am J. Nursing,* pp. 1436-40, September 1976.

15. Freud, S. "A Child Is Being Beaten." *Sexuality and the Psychology of Love.* Coll. Papers. New York: Collier Books, p. 109, 1963.

16. Freud, S. "A Case of Homosexuality in a Woman." *Sexuality and the Psychology of Love.* Coll. Papers. New York: Collier Books, pp. 149-154, 1963.

17. Winnicott, D. W. "Transitional Objects and Transitional Phenomena—A Study of the First Not-Me Possession." *Int. J. of P.S.A.* 34: 1-9, 1953.

18. Marder, L. "Psychiatric Experience with a Liberalized Therapeutic Abortion Law." *Amer. J. Psychiat.* 126:9: 1230-36, March 1970.

19. Bernstein, I. C. "Psychiatric Indications for Therapeutic Abortion." Symposium on Therapeutic Abortion. *MN Med.* January 1967.

20. Belsey, E. M., et al. "Predictive Factors in Emotional Response to Abortion." *Soc. Sci. and Med.* 1171-2, 1977.

21. Fisher, H. W., et al. "Pregnancy Fantasies." *MN Med.* pp. 129-31, February 1974.

Pregnancy and Sexual Assault

Sandra Kathleen Mahkorn

Rape! The very word is a symbol of violence and vulnerability for most women. It is a sudden, shattering intrusion which can leave the victim with deep physical, emotional, and psychological scars that are aggravated by a society which often sees her as the guilty party. Believing that she is dirty, ugly, and dehumanized and knowing that many will view her either as pitiful and helpless or as defiled and disgusting, she often takes great pains to conceal the fact of the assault.

Perhaps the greatest problems the sexual assault victim must confront emanate from the lingering myths about rape and the circumstances and individuals involved. Unfortunate and erroneous beliefs that rape is confined to "bad" neighborhoods, "immoral" nightspots or only happens if the woman allows it to happen have been a major target of several community education projects. Although regrettable, it is not surprising that many of these misconceptions have persisted. Until recently, the vast majority of literature on the subject of rape dealt primarily with areas relating to criminology, and the traits and characteristics of the rapist,[5] while allowing certain prejudices to continue. Concentration on the characteristics of the criminal has been the case with other crimes as well. Finally, however, victims and their special needs are receiving some long overdue attention.

Myths About Rape and Pregnancy

Intrinsic to an understanding of the crisis confronting a woman who becomes pregnant as a result of rape is a non-biased view of the victim and of the rape act itself. Somehow related to the mistaken notion that a woman is responsible for, or is able to prevent the attack is the belief that rape is a sex crime. Many states still regrettably categorize rape as a crime against sexual morality. Others, as a result of abundant evidence which de-

emphasized the sexual motivation for the attack,[14][32] have reclassi-
fied rape as a crime of sexual assault. The essential aspect of violence in sexual assault is affirmed by Herzig, who defines rape as
"an expression of a violent act; it is a victimization of a person
against his or her will, with sex as a component."[17] Such an understanding of sexual assault finds its origin in Roman law which defined rape as a "crime of force, (*crimen vis*)."[34] Groth, et al., investigated three components of sexual assault; namely, power, anger,
and sexuality. The authors found that "either power or anger dom-
inates and that rape, rather than being primarily an expression of
sexual desire, is, in fact, the use of sexuality to express issues of
power and anger."[14] The central element of violence can be observed in the victim's reactions as well. "For example, fear of dying
is commonly the most terrifying aspect of the sexual assault reported by rape victims."[24] Schaefer, et al., state that rape is considered a life-threatening experience by most victims.[30]

Despite abundant evidence to the contrary, the sexual aspect
of rape appears to receive overwhelming attention in the minds of
most individuals. Barnett and Feild found that 88 percent of both
men and women college students agreed with the statement,
"Rape is a sex crime," and that 32 percent of the women and 48
percent of the men surveyed agreed with the statement, "The reason most rapists commit rape is for sex."[3] Notman and Nadelson
point out that the emphasis on the sexual nature of the act and
minimization of the violence contributes to the victim's unwarranted sense of guilt. "Since long-standing sexual taboos still per-
sist for many people, even an unwilling participant in a sexual act
is accused and depreciated."[27] This phenomenon of "blaming the
victim" seems to be unprecedented in other criminal activities
and is a major factor in the unique emotional reactions of the sexual assualt victim as opposed to victims of other crimes. One
would not, for example, feel that a man whose car was stolen was
responsible for the crime simply because he decided to visit a
friend who lived in a high crime neighborhood. However, many
seem to be much less reluctant to accuse a rape victim of being in
the wrong place at the wrong time. These attitudes are also reflected in the Barnett and Feild survey in which 27 percent of the wom-
en and 41 percent of the men agreed with the statement, "A woman should be responsible for preventing her victimization in a
rape."[3] In an effort to explain the motivation behind blaming the
victim, Abarbanel writes,

> There is a self-serving comfort in promulgating this
> belief. Blame is a form of control—it distances and
> protects us, and masks our own shared vulnerabil-
> ity.[1]

The victim's feelings of guilt, shame, and responsibility are encouraged by such attitudes,[5] compelling her to conceal the incident. Pregnancy prevents such concealment, and because of these provincial attitudes it can compound the crisis the woman faces.

In my experience as a sexual assault counselor, feelings of guilt were extremely common and usually quite irrational. However, the "socialization to the attitude of 'blame the victim' "[5] often compelled the woman to actively search for personal characteristics and events through which she could claim responsibility for the assault. For example, at one point I was working with two victims of separate attacks who attributed the assault to their personal appearances. One felt responsible because she wore make-up and believed she was attractive while the second victim was convinced that she was unattractive and that it was because of this that she was raped.

Perhaps more of a gross exaggeration than a myth is the mistaken and unfortunate belief that pregnancy is a frequent complication of sexual assault. This is emphatically not the case, and there are several medically sound reasons for it.[31] First, it is important to note that rape is legally defined as sexual intercourse, and only penetration, not ejaculation, is necessary for rape to have occurred.[9] In one study of 500 rape victims, "Spermatozoa were identified on the fixed smears from 306, or 61 percent" of the patients,[9] whereas another study identified spermatozoa in only 52 percent.[10]   In yet a third study, Groth and Burgess report,

> [O]f the 69 women for whom we have complete data on the presence or absence of sperm, clinical evidence for sperm was found in only 32 cases. This statistic is even more impressive when one looks at the number of women raped by more than one man. Half the 23 victims who encountered multiple rapists had negative laboratory tests for sperm.[15]

Second, perhaps somewhat related to this first point, is the finding that there is a relatively higher rate of sexual dysfunction in sexual assault. Groth and Burgess found some type of sexual dysfunction among 57 percent of 101 cases for which the presence or absence of dysfunction could be evaluated.[15] They point out that "convicted offenders' physiologic reactions during rape reveal an impressively high rate of erective and ejaculatory dysfunction at some point during the actual assault."[15] Perhaps an even more striking finding which differentiates the rapist from the normal is the high incidence of retarded ejaculation, described as a "difficulty or failure to ejaculate during intercourse,"[15] which was reported in 26 of these cases. However, the retarded ejaculation in the general population is a complaint of only 1 in 700 men.[16]

Third, there are various medical factors related to the victim herself which minimize the possibility of pregnancy. Included among these are sterility, a previous hysterectomy, the use of contraceptives or an IUD, and the wide age range of rape victims. For example, in one study of 117 victims, no patients were known to have become pregnant as a result of the assault, despite the fact that only 17 of this number had been given anti-implantation medication, such as DES (diethylstilbestrol).[11] Reasons for this included the fact that 23 were taking oral contraceptives, had an IUD in place or had previously had a tubal ligation. Another 49 had no medical risk of pregnancy because of an already present pregnancy, a previous hysterectomy, pelvic radiation, or the fact that the victims were either postmenopausal or had not reached menarche.[11] Added to this evidence is the finding that even a woman raped on the very day she ovulates has only a one in ten chance of pregnancy.[31]

The evidence presented, therefore, supports the conclusion that pregnancy is a rare complication of rape. Hayman and Lanza reported a frequency of pregnancy resulting from rape in only 0.6 percent of 2190 victims,[19] while three times that many were already pregnant at the time of the attack. Other authors[13] report dramatically lower rates of pregnancy from sexual assault.

Ignorance about fertility patterns and sex, the highly emotionally charged nature of the issue, and an exaggeration of the things we fear have resulted in terrifying misconceptions about pregnancy resulting from rape adhered to by both society and victim. For example, Fox and Scherl report an incident in which the victim was unusually anxious about becoming pregnant because "she had thought all intercourse resulted in pregnancy."[12] Fear, too, has contributed to an exaggeration of the frequency of rape. As a result of responses received from female medical students, McGuire and Stern concluded, "The general tendency in female responses was . . . to overestimate the incidence."[26] For the same reasons, fear probably contributes to the exaggeration of the frequency of pregnancy resulting from rape.

An unfortunate but realistic possibility accounting for the seeming encouragement of abortion of a pregnancy resulting from rape evolves from racial prejudices and myths about the racial makeup of attacker and victim. Contrary to some widespread fears which conjure up images of black attackers and white victims, it should be noted that in 70 percent to 90 percent of sexual assault cases the rapist and victim are of the same race.[29]

Not only for the peace of mind of the victim but for the enlightenment of the general population, community education efforts should be directed towards the dissipation of these myths and misconceptions.

The Pregnant Sexual Assault Victim—A Profile

It is not the intent of this study to infer that because pregnancy as a result of sexual assault is indeed rare, this issue can be ignored. On the contrary, in a fraction of a percent of rape cases, pregnancy does occur, and it is a matter to be seriously and sympathetically addressed. The special fears, attitudes, emotions, and needs of the woman pregnant as a result of sexual assault must be carefully examined and understood in order to aid her in supporting the unborn child through his or her birth. It would be naive to deny the existence of additional emotional conflicts or to believe that such a pregnancy is in any way easy. However, I know both from personal experience and as a result of the present study that with sensitive support such burdens can be lessened.

Method

Questionnaires, concerning contacts with women who reported becoming pregnant as a result of sexual assault, were sent to various counseling and social welfare agencies that are known for assisting women through problem pregnancies. Questions were designed to elicit statistical information about women who reported becoming pregnant as a result of sexual assault. In addition, open-ended questions were asked regarding the victims' reasons for continuing the pregnancy, the special needs of pregnant rape victims, the conditions which make continuation of a pregnancy difficult in this situation, and the kinds of support and services that are necessary in aiding a pregnant sexual assault victim through her pregnancy. Counselors were asked to relay their client's images, feelings, attitudes, or beliefs about the fetus or unborn child and describe in what way, if any, these changed as the pregnancy progressed.

Respondents also rated clients on a seven-point scale on levels of eight common human emotions or conditions at the time of their initial and final contacts with the client. Lower ratings on these scales indicated a progressively more unhealthy condition, while higher ratings indicated progressively healthier conditions, with a rating of four representing the mid-point.

Responses to questions were tabulated, categorized, and

summarized. Mean scores for each of the eight conditions or emotions were tabulated for the time of the initial contact and the last contact with the counselor. The mean differences for each condition or emotion between the initial and final contacts were also computed.

Results

There was a more than 30 percent return of the questionnaires, with 15 of the agencies claiming contacts with women who reported becoming pregnant as a result of sexual assault. The remaining 16 reported one or more contacts with women making this claim. These 16 respondents acknowledged being contacted by a total of 37 individuals reporting to have become pregnant as a result of rape. Of these, 28 chose to continue their pregnancies, 5 chose abortion and the outcome for the remaining 4 could not be determined.

Of the 28 choosing to continue their pregnancies, 17 chose adoption, 3 chose to keep the child; for the remaining 8, the outcome was unknown. Eight of a total of 37 victims were known to have reported the attack to legal authorities, in other words, the police or district attorney. Sixteen did not report the attack; for the remaining 13, this information could not be determined.

Responses to the question, "Of those sexual assault victims choosing to continue their pregnancies, what factors did these clients mention as being most important in their decision not to seek an abortion?" fell into four main categories which are listed in Table 1.

Table 1

	Number of Responses	% of Responses
Category I Viewed abortion as killing, immoral, or an act of violence	6	37.5
Category II Denial, or lack of realization of pregnancy until after the first trimester	4	25.0
Category III Belief that the unborn child had an intrinsic meaning or purpose	2	12.5
Category IV Other	4	25.0
Total	16	100.0

A belief that abortion involved violence, killing or was immoral (Category I) was the reason most frequently reported for clients' decisions against abortion. Counselors report that victims who were "anti-abortion" felt that abortion was a "violent way of ending a human life" and believed, for example, that abortion was "killing."

Category II (Denial of pregnancy until after first trimester) is self-explanatory.

Those who reported having clients who felt the fetus or unborn child had an intrinsic meaning or purpose (Category III) related clients' viewpoints such as "All life has meaning" and "This child can bring love and happiness into someone's life."

Category IV (Other) included statements like the client "never considered abortion to our knowledge," and "psychologically she felt she would suffer more mental anguish from taking the life of the unborn child than carrying the baby to term."

Nine respondents replied to the question, "Do women who become pregnant as a result of sexual assault have needs which are greater than or different from other women faced with a problem pregnancy?" There were 8 affirmative responses, no negative responses and 1 respondent who felt that her experience was "too limited" to make this determination. The counselors were asked to list these different and greater needs and each response was placed in one of four categories listed in Table 2.

Thirteen of a total of 26, or 50 percent of the responses to this question, dealt with the pregnant victim's need to confront "feelings or issues related to the rape experience" (Category I). This category included emotional reactions which various authors report as being frequent among sexual assault victims. For example, counselors believed it was important to deal with "feelings of guilt—blame—what did I do," with a "fear" of the "sex act or men," and with "low sexual esteem—feeling dirty—defiled." Also listed as Category I responses are statements such as "anger toward attacker needs ventilation," and "denial of the rape experience . . . must be dealt with."

Category II (Needs similar to but greater than the needs of other women with problem pregnancies) is self-explanatory.

Category III (Need to confront and explore feelings about the pregnancy and fetus or unborn child) responses consisted of 19 percent of the responses and were related to statements reflecting the need to confront "resentment of the pregnancy," "hostility towards child," and "denial of the . . . pregnancy."

Responses classified as "Other" (Category IV) related to emotional responses that were not as easily directly attributable to the assault and with needs particular to a certain client such as the need for "defense against the attacker."

Responses to the question, "From your experience, what factors, conditions or situations do you believe make it most difficult for a woman who is pregnant as a result of sexual assault to continue her pregnancy?" fell into five categories which are listed in Table 3.

Category I (Opinions, attitudes and beliefs of others about the rape and pregnancy) responses were most frequently mentioned and are characterized by counselor statements such as, "family pressure," the victim's belief that "people will not believe that she was raped or that it could have been prevented," and "boyfriend's" attitude.

Category II responses referred to the pregnancy as being a "continual reminder of the rape event" and reflect statements such as "the presence of the baby is a constant reminder of the 'nightmare.' "

Category III (Fear, anger and other feelings about the attacker) responses typify statements such as "hate or fear of the baby's father," while Category IV (Negative feelings about self) relate to feelings of "guilt" or low "sexual self-esteem," for example.

In 21 cases, counselors reported having contact with the pregnant sexual assault victim through the birth of the child.* Two of these cases were eliminated for the purpose of this study because of incomplete data. Questions to ascertain each "client's images, feelings, attitudes, or beliefs about the fetus or unborn child at the time of the initial contact" were asked. The respondent was also requested to report whether any of these images, feelings, attitudes, or beliefs changed, and, if so, in what way they changed. Of the 19 clients considered in this study, 12 were reported to have changed and 7 were reported to have maintained their viewpoints and perspectives of the fetus or unborn child.

Four separate individuals independently rated the respondents' answers to the question, "To the best of your knowledge, what were the client's images, feelings, attitudes or beliefs about the fetus or unborn child at the time of your initial contact?" Responses were categorized as to whether they constituted a negative or positive view on the part of the client. In the case of the 12 clients who were reported to have in some way changed their viewpoints, raters were asked to state whether the change was (1) from one positive viewpoint to another, (2) from a negative to a more positive viewpoint, (3) from a positive to a more negative viewpoint, or (4) from one negative viewpoint to another.

---

* In one case the child was due the same month the questionnaire was completed.

Table 2

	Number of Responses	% of Responses (to tenths)
Category I Need to deal with feelings or issues related to the rape experience, such as anger, fear, and sexual problems	13	50.0
Category II Needs of pregnant rape victim are similar to, but greater than the needs of other women with problem pregnancies	3	11.5
Category III Need to explore and confront feelings about the pregnancy and fetus or unborn child	5	19.2
Category IV Other	5	19.2
Total	26	100.0

Table 3

	Number of Responses	% of Responses (to tenths)
Category I Opinions, attitudes, and beliefs of others about the rape and pregnancy	4	28.6
Category II The pregnancy serves as a continual reminder of the rape event	2	14.3
Category III Fear, anger and other feelings about the attacker	2	14.3
Category IV Negative feelings about self (e.g. self-esteem, guilt)	2	14.3
Category V Other	4	28.6
Total	14	100.0

Figure 1

Mean rankings for initial and final client contacts for 19 subjects for various emotions and conditions. Rankings were determined by counselor-respondents.

☐ Rankings for initial contacts
■ Rankings for final contacts

	Self-Esteem	Anxiety	Anger	Fear	Satisfaction with Present Life Situation	Loneliness (Isolation)*	Depression	Contented-ness**
top	7— very high	non-existent	non-existent	non-existent	total	none	none	extreme
initial	4.84	5.26	5.26	5.05	4.95	4.56	5.16	4.56
final	3.16	2.26	3.00	2.16	3.42	3.88	3.05	2.44
bottom	1— very low	extreme	extreme	extreme	none	extreme	extreme	none

Scale: 7, 6, 5, 4, 3, 2, 1

*18 subjects
**16 subjects

Table 4

Clients whose viewpoints were reported to have changed
during the counselor-client relationship.
(Total of 12, 2 not classifiable)

Changing from one positive viewpoint to another   2
   Example: "It was a baby, it needed a good home"
          to
   "accepted herself and pregnancy better"

Changing from a negative to a more positive viewpoint   7
   Example: "Had 'no feelings' about the baby"
          to
   "realized she loved it and decided to keep the baby."

Changing from a positive to a more negative viewpoint   0

Changing from one negative viewpoint to another   1
   Example: "Displayed anger toward the fetus"
          to
   "less angry, more depressed"

Clients whose viewpoints were reported not to have changed during the
counselor-client relationship.
(Total of 7, 1 not classifiable)

Consistently positive viewpoint   2
   Example: "God has his meaning for all of life"

Consistently negative viewpoint   4
   Example: "Feared it would look like the father"

Table 5

Mean of final rankings minus initial rankings for 8 conditions
and emotions for 19 clients.

Variable	Mean Differences
Self-Esteem	+1.68
Anxiety	+3.00
Anger	+2.26
Fear	+2.89
Satisfaction with Present Life Situation	+1.53
Loneliness (Isolation)*	+0.72
Depression	+2.11
Contentedness**	+2.13

*18 subjects
**16 subjects
Note: Positive numbers indicate progressively healthier change. Negative numbers
indicate progressively unhealthier change.

For the 7 cases in which no change was reported, raters were asked to determine whether the initial images, feelings, attitudes, or beliefs were positive or negative. Examples of positive viewpoints included increased acceptance or decreased hostility toward the unborn child or fetus; emotional attachment or concern for the unborn; a recognition of the child's intrinsic meaning or purpose; a realization that the child was a blameless victim; an awareness and acceptance of responsibility for the fetus' well-being; and the realization that the child was "normal." Examples of negative responses included statements reflecting hostility, resentment, or anger toward the child; anxiety or fear that the child would be malformed or "look like the father"; denial of the pregnancy; and a lack of any sense of attachment or feeling for the fetus or unborn child. Only those cases for which at least three of the four raters were in agreement were categorized, while those cases for which less than a 75 percent agreement was reached were defined as not classifiable. These results are summarized in Table 4.

None of the clients were viewed as changing from a positive to a more negative perspective of the fetus by any of the raters. Of the 12 who were reported to have changed their images, attitudes, feelings, and beliefs about the fetus, 8 were found to have come to a more positive viewpoint, one changed from one positive attitude to a different positive attitude, 2 were not classifiable, and one was believed to have changed from one to another negative viewpoint.

Of the 7 respondents claiming no change in their clients' viewpoints, raters felt that 4 of these clients had positive viewpoints, 2 had negative viewpoints, and one was not classifiable. Counselors were also asked to rate their clients on a scale of 1 to 7 for eight human emotions or conditions. Levels were to be assessed both for the time of the initial contact, and for the most recent contact with the pregnant rape victim. Mean rankings for each emotion or condition for both the initial and final contact were computed and are illustrated in Figure 1. In addition, change in either a healthy or unhealthy direction was assessed by computing the mean of the difference between the initial and final contacts for each of the emotions or conditions shown in Figure 1. There were no mean shifts in unhealthy directions as is illustrated in Table 5. The greatest mean shift, positive or healthy improvement, was observed for ratings of fear and anxiety respectively, while the lowest mean progression was seen for ratings of loneliness.

Discussion and Conclusions

A number of conclusions can be drawn from the data present-ed in this study. It is interesting to note that the reporting rate, that is, the number of pregnant sexual assault victims who reported the attack to legal authorities, reflects the national estimates of the number who report versus those who fail to do so. In the present study, 8 of a total of 37, or 21.6 percent, were known to have reported the attack, although for 16 of the 37 victims this information could not be determined.

Various national estimates of the reporting frequency are generally between 1 in 5[29] and 1 in 4.5.[2] Reasons postulated for the reluctance to report are numerous and varied. Abarbanel believes that these include feelings of guilt and shame, ignorance of the proper procedure in reporting, fear of unsympathetic treatment by various agencies as well as family and friends, and lack of knowledge about various community services.[1] Because of these common fears and misunderstandings, the view that a pregnant rape victim who failed to report the incident probably was not raped cannot be supported.

The possibility exists that some of the women in this study were pregnant at the time of the assult or became pregnant shortly after the assult as a result of sexual relations with husbands or boyfriends. However, even if this is in fact the case for some of the victims, because they believed the pregnancy was a result of the assault, it seems safe to assume that emotional reactions would be similar to women impregnated by the attacker.

The fact that abortion was viewed by many pregnant assault victims as killing, immoral or an act of violence is significant. Because it is likely that the victim already harbors feelings of guilt as a result of the assault, medico-social pressures which encourage and result in abortion could compound the woman's feelings of guilt and self-blame. Guilt feelings such as these are not to be dismissed as childish or neurotic. Clemens and Smith write that "the counselor who views moral-religious guilt as anything except normal guilt in the American culture would be characterized by naivete and/or bias."[8] Perhaps as a result of their own biases and an unwillingness to deal with the more emotionally difficult complications of a pregnant rape victim, many physicians suggest abortion in this case, as one would prescribe aspirin for a tension headache. For example, Hunt writes:

> We advise *all* rape victims that if they miss their next regular period by more than one week, they *should* return for *menstrual extraction* or *suction curettage*. (Emphasis added)[21]

While on the surface this "suggestion" may appear acceptable and even "humane" to many, the victim is dealt another disservice. Such condescending attitudes on the part of physicians, friends, and family can only serve to reaffirm the sense of helplessness and vulnerability that was so violently conveyed in the act of sexual assault itself. At a time when she is struggling to regain her sense of self-esteem, such a "take charge" attitude can be especially damaging. Often the offer of such "quick and easy" solutions as abortion only serve those who are uncomfortable or unwilling to deal with the special problems and needs that such complications as pregnancy might present.

The effect of societal beliefs about rape, attitudes directly or indirectly communicated by family and friends, and the impact such viewpoints may have on the victim, especially the victim who becomes pregnant as a result of the assault, cannot be ignored. Rosner points out, "The most damaging results of a rape can be the covert or sometimes even overt rejection and accusing attitudes which are often seen on the part of family or friends."[29] Opinions, attitudes, and beliefs of others about the rape and pregnancy were reasons most commonly mentioned by respondents as conditions or situations which "make it most difficult for a woman who is pregnant as a result of sexual assault to continue her pregnancy" (see Table 3).

There are three relatively common reactions of family and friends, sometimes subtly and unconsciously conveyed, which encourage the victim's sense of shame and self-blame. She is made to feel that she has "sinned" and that she must at all costs conceal that "sin." Such provincial views lead the victim to the unfortunate conclusion that abortion is the only solution.

First, anger may be openly or indirectly communicated to the victim. Such anger arises from the accusatory viewpoint that "nice women don't get raped" or that the victim must have done something to provoke the attack.[33]

Second, either because of significant others' discomfort in discussing the situation, or because of a belief that such a tragedy somehow reflects badly on the family, great pains may be taken to avoid or conceal the event.

> Often her relatives and friends try to dissuade her from thinking or talking about it (the assault) in the mistaken belief that she will become more emotionally distressed. However, if others refuse to listen, the patient may conclude that they are embarrassed and ashamed and want to punish her for what has happened.[12]

This was an especially difficult problem for one of my own clients who had become pregnant as a result of sexual assault. The family, although well-meaning in the belief that it was best to forget the incident and even the pregnancy, failed to recognize that the victim had a real need to discuss her feelings and fears with people who cared about her. Elizabeth Kubler-Ross had noted similar difficulties in communication between family members and dying patients.[25] The rape experience and the experience of death and dying may be similar in that they both awaken a sense of vulnerability and are both difficult to confront.

The third unhealthy attitude conveyed by friends and family is that the woman is somehow "tainted" or "dirtied" as a result of her tragic experience. "Often they may feel that the woman has been 'ruined' and may convey this to her so strongly that it becomes part of her self image."[12] This attitude often evolves from the dehumanizing belief that the woman "belongs to" or is "the property of" a man and that his "merchandise" has in some way been made "unclean."

> A husband described feeling physically disgusted when approaching his "unclean" wife sexually, immediately following her rape. Obviously such responses may reinforce the victim's sense of humiliation and devaluation.[33]

It is not extraordinary to assume that these negative views about the victim will be transferred to the unborn child as well. In fact the pregnancy itself could be viewed by such individuals as a symbol of the woman having been "touched." Brownmiller reports that Bengali women who had become pregnant as a result of being raped by Pakistani soldiers in 1971 were rejected by their husbands with the reasoning that "no Moslem husband would take back a wife who had been touched by another man, even if she had been subdued by force."[7] Thus, it should be apparent that much of the trauma arising from a rape resulting in pregnancy must be attributed to ignorance, misunderstanding, and suspicions about the nature of this criminal act and to condescending attitudes toward the victim.

In addition, many, because of the ugliness and brutality of rape, fail to recognize the humanity and uniqueness of the unborn child. By condoning such attitudes we are telling the pregnant rape victim that the life she carries is repulsive. No wonder abortion—a violent act—may seem like the only solution. Violence is thus justified as the most "effective" and "efficient" solution. But such negative solutions must be rejected. Instead, we must be courageous enough as a society to address some of the deeper roots of the problem, namely, our own ignorance and prejudice.

One of the respondents in the present study pointed out that the "largest and most commanding factor" which makes it most difficult for a pregnant rape victim to continue her pregnancy is "that people will not believe that she was raped" or will think "that it could have been prevented, and that she would have to repeat her story so many times."

The central issue, then, should not be whether we can abort all pregnant sexual assault victims, but rather an exploration of the things we can change in ourselves, and through community education, to support such women through their pregnancies. The "abortion is the best solution" approach can only serve to encourage the belief that sexual assault is something for which the victim must bear shame—a sin to be carefully concealed.

Fifty percent of the responses to the question relating to the special needs of pregnant sexual assault victims dealt with the importance of addressing feelings or issues related to the rape experience (see Table 2). This supports the conclusion that painful emotions associated with the assault may be of greater importance than feelings related to the pregnancy and fetus (see Category III, Table 2). One social worker respondent commented:

> [T]his woman had to research issues on her own
> . . . she was a Ph.D. candidate and was able to continue her studies despite the pregnancy . . . I think the reason she returned to me was that in the initial contact I was able to let her know that the pregnancy was not her main problem.

This has been true of my own experience as well. Perhaps too often the pregnancy receives the most attention and the anger, guilt, fear, and lower self-esteem related to the assault fail to be addressed.

Very significantly, it was noted in the results that none of the clients were viewed as changing from a more positive to a more negative image or attitude about the fetus. On the contrary, 63 percent of the clients were rated either as having changed from negative to more positive images, attitudes, beliefs, or feelings about the unborn child or as having a positive viewpoint to begin with. It appears, then, that while there may be some initial tendency to associate the fetus with the often-feared father or with the brutal attack, such association will usually change towards more positive perspectives. It has been my experience that the pregnant victim becomes progressively aware of the individuality and innocence of the fetus or unborn child.

In addition to these positive changes, Figure 1 and Table 5 suggest that, with supportive counseling, healthy changes are the rule rather than the exception. Indeed, for none of the conditions or emotions evaluated was there a mean negative change. Also worthy of mention is the fact that there was the least degree of healthy progression for the variable of loneliness. This may support the conclusion mentioned earlier, that the attitudes projected by others and not the pregnancy itself pose the central problem for the pregnant victim.

By no means am I attempting to conclude that pregnancy as a result of rape is a simple matter. Such a conclusion would indeed be naive. This study does seem to suggest, however, that even though emotionally and psychologically difficult, these burdens can be lessened with proper support.

Anger is a frequent aftermath of the assault. Even if the attacker is prosecuted, this anger is seldom fully ventilated. Yet these feelings are important to address, since they may otherwise be directed in unhealthy ways. For example, Fox and Scherl mention that, "Frequently her anger toward the assailant is distorted into anger toward herself . . . ."[12] Anger, under these circumstances, is certainly easy to understand, but not always so simple to deal with. In New York, Inez Garcia sought out and killed the man who aided in raping her. She was sentenced to five years to life imprisonment. It is also understandable that such anger may be displaced on an unborn child in the decision for abortion. These examples represent unhealthy ways of coping with such feelings. One counselor-respondent wrote:

> [T]he client was hostile about her pregnancy, felt guilty about the rape, and displayed anger towards the unborn child, *initially*. At one point she beat her fists on her swollen abdomen to try to miscarry. (Emphasis added)

Such reactions may not be acceptable, but one may sympathize with the motivation behind these actions. "No one person has a right to decide on the life or death of another person. Yet, there are circumstances where murder is understandable . . . ."[32]

Our understanding of ourselves as civilized beings depends on our embrace of compassionate solutions and our rejection of violence as justifiable revenge.

References

1. Abarbanel, Gail. "Helping Victims of Rape." *Social Work*, 21 (1976), 478-482.

2. Abarbanel, Gail. "Helping Victims of Rape," citing the study by Ennis, Philip H. *Criminal Victimization in the United States: A Report of a National Survey.* President's Commission on Law Enforcement and Administration of Justice. Washington, D.C.: National Opinion Research Center, 1967; U.S. Department of Justice, Law Enforcement Assistance Administration. *Criminal Victimization in the United States, 1973, Advance Report.* Washington,D.C.: U.S. Government Printing Office, 1975.

3. Barnett, Nona J., and Feild, Hubert S. "Sex Differences in University Students' Attitudes towards Rape." *J. College Student Personnel,* 18 (1977), 93-96.

4. Burgess, Ann Wolbert, and Holmstrom, Lynda Lytle. "Coping Behavior of the Rape Victim." *Amer. J. Psychiat.*, 133, No. 4 (1976), 413-417.

5. Burgess, Ann Wolbert, and Holmstrom, Lynda Lytle. "Rape Trauma Syndrome." *Amer. J. Psychiat.*, 131, No. 9 (1974), 981-986.

6. Burgess, Ann Wolbert, and Holmstrom, Lynda Lytle. *Rape: Victims of Crisis.* Bowie, Maryland: Robert J. Brady Co., 1974.

7. Brownmiller, Susan. *Against Our Will.* New York: Simon and Schuster, 1975.

8. Clemens, Bryan T., and Smith, Darrell. *The Counselor and Religious Questioning and Conflicts.* Boston: Houghton Mifflin Co., 1973.

9. Dahlke, Miriam, et al. "Identification of Semen in 500 Patients Seen Because of Rape." *Amer. J. Clin. Path.*, 68, No. 6 (1977), 740-746.

10. Dahlke, Miriam, et al. "Identification of Semen in 500 Patients Seen Because of Rape," citing the study by Gomez, R. R.; Wunsch, C. D.; Davis, J. H., et al. "Qualitative and Quantitative Determinations of Acid Phosphatase Activity in Vaginal Washings." *Amer. J. Clin. Path.*, 63 (1975), 423-432.

11. Everett, Royice B., and Jimerson, Gordon K. "The Rape Victim: A Review of 117 Consecutive Cases." *Obstetrics and Gynecology,* 50, No. 1 (1977), 88-90.

12. Fox, Sandra Sutherland, and Scherl, Donald J. "Crisis Intervention with Victims of Rape." *Social Work,* 17 (1972), 37-42.

13. Gerster, Carolyn F. "Why Not Keep Legalized Abortion for Rape and Incest?" *Nat. Right to Life News,* Nov. 1975, p. 13.

14. Groth, A. Nicholas; Burgess, Ann Wolbert; and Holmstrom, Lynda Lytle. "Rape: Power, Anger, and Sexuality." *Amer. J. Psychiat.*, 134, No. 11 (1977), 1239-1243.

15. Groth, A. Nicholas, and Burgess, Ann Wolbert. "Sexual Dysfunction During Rape." *New England J. Med.,* 297, No. 14 (1977), 764-766.

16. Katchadourian, H. A., and Lunde, D. T. *Fundamentals of Human Sexuality.* New York: Holt, Rinehart and Winston, 1972.

17. Herzig, Norman. "Some Thoughts About Rape." *Montefiore Med.,* 2, No. 1 (1977), 14-16.

18. Hilberman, Elaine. *The Rape Victim.* New York: Basic Books Inc., 1976.

19. Hilberman, Elaine. *The Rape Victim,* citing the study by Hayman, C. R., and Lanza, C. "Sexual Assault on Women and Girls." *Amer. J. Obstetrics and Gynecology,* 109, No. 3 (1971), 480-486.

20. Holmstrom, Lynda Lytle, and Burgess, Ann Wolbert. *The Victim of Rape: Institutional Reactions.* New York: John Wiley and Sons, 1978.

21. Hunt, Glenn R. "Rape: An Organized Approach to Evaluation and Treatment." *Amer. Family Physician,* 15, No. 1 (1977), 154-158.

22. Hursch, Carolyn J. *The Trouble with Rape.* Chicago: Nelson-Hall, 1977.

23. Joe, Victor C.; McGee, Shanna J.; and Dazey, Darryl. "Religiousness and Devaluation of the Rape Victim." *J. Clin. Psychiat.,* 33, No. 1 (1977), 64.

24. Kaufman, Arthur, et al. "Follow-up of Rape Victims in a Family Practice Setting." *Southern Med. J.,* 69, No. 12 (1976), 1569-1571.

25. Kübler-Ross, Elizabeth. *On Death and Dying.* New York: Mac-Millan Publishing Co., 1969.

26. McGuire, L. S., and Stern, Michael. "Survey of Incidence of and Physicians' Attitudes toward Sexual Assault." *Public Health Reports,* 91, No. 2 (1976), 103-109.

27. Notman, Malkah, and Nadelson, Carol. "The Rape Victim: Psychodynamic Considerations." *Amer. J. Psychiat.,* No. 4 (1976) 408-412.

28. Robinson, G. Erlick. "Management of the Rape Victim." *Canadian Med. Assoc. J.,* 115 (1976), 520-522.

29. Rosner, Bennett. "Thoughts by a Psychiatrist on Rape." *Montefiore Med.,* 2, No. 1 (1977), 15, 17.

30. Schaefer, Joanne; Sullivan, Rebecca A.; and Goldstein, Frank L. "Counseling Sexual Abuse Victims." *Amer. Family Physician,* 18, No. 5 (1978), 85-91.

31. Seltzer, Vicki. "Medical Management of the Rape Victim." *J. Amer. Med. Women's Assoc.*, 32, No. 4 (1977), 141-144.

32. Shainess, Natalie. "Psychological Significance of Rape." *New York State J. Med.*, 76, No. 12 (1976), 2044-2048.

33. Silverman, Daniel C. "Sharing the Crisis of Rape." *Amer. J. Orthopsychiatry*, 48, No. 1 (1978), 166-173.

34. Tabori, Paul. *The Social History of Rape.* London: The New English Library Ltd., 1971.

The Consequences of Incest: Giving and Taking Life

George E. Maloof, M.D.

I. Life-giving: Pregnancy

Teenage Pregnancy

Before looking specifically at incestuous pregnancies that offer new life in a decadent situation, let us look briefly at the issue of teenage pregnancies in general. In recent years birth rates have declined for all age groups except teenagers,[1] and the increase in teenage pregnancy has become the battle-cry of the population explosion alarmists of the sixties who generally have been defused.[2] Studies have revealed that such girls tend to have a low self-image compared to girls who do not become pregnant,[3] and suffer from a lack of close relationship with a caring adult.[4] At a meeting convened by the Department of Health, Education, and Welfare on January 26, 1978, to consider ways of preventing adolescent pregnancies, Dr. David Allen of the Life Support Center at Johns Hopkins Hospital showed that "an ongoing relationship with specially assigned doctors and center personnel markedly reduced the numbers of young women who became pregnant a second time out of wedlock."[5] Since the lack of a supportive adult figure leads to the pregnancy and the presence of such a person prevents a pregnancy, it would seem that the girl is actually looking for a relationship with an adult rather than a baby when she becomes pregnant. In a classic study of 100 pregnant girls the baby simply became a way of reconnecting with a formerly rejecting parent for 70 percent of them. For these girls, all of whom suffered from poor interpersonal relations, the babies held out hope for a better human relationship with someone.[6]

For a society that has generally become more tolerant of genital arousal activity at any age and with anybody, the one remaining taboo is becoming pregnant. Yet even this is becoming socially acceptable or even "very much of a status symbol"[7] among teenagers, particularly in California, which leads the nation in illegitimacy and teenage pregnancies.[8] The problem of the pregnant teenager is epitomized when the girl's parent rationalizes that, "Sex relations are not as serious at eight years old, because then girls can't have babies."[9] The same maternal concern might have been expressed a few years later by the mother who exclaimed with relief to a child counselor regarding her husband and daughter's incest, "Thank God, she's still a virgin, he only sodomized her."[10] In neither situation is pregnancy likely to occur; yet in both cases there is little parental protection of the girl's sexual integrity. If pregnancy is the only violation of the girl's sexual integrity which will rouse the mother to care for her daughter, then "so be it."

Incestuous Pregnancies

Incidence

Before discussing specifically the social situation of incestuous pregnancies as a particular type of illegitimate teenage pregnancy, let us look at some figures indicating the incidence of such pregnancies. Considering the prevalence of teenage pregnancies in general, incest treatment programs uniformly marvel at the low incidence of pregnancies from incest. Barbara Myers, who has worked with 400 women in the Christopher Street program in Minneapolis, reports a 1 percent pregnancy rate. She has noted that years of incestuous coital relations appear to be associated with cessation of menses, which resumes after the girls enter the therapy program.[11]

> The great fear of pregnancy expressed by these
> girls may affect their fertility, as perhaps happens
> with rape victims, studies of which have revealed
> no pregnancies occurring.[12]

Henry Giarretto, whose incest program in Santa Clara County has treated 1500 families, reports a less than 1 percent incidence.[13] And Peter Coleman, in Washington State, reports no pregnancies from the incestuous relationship itself.[14]

The extremely low incidence of incestuous pregnancies found in currently active incest treatment programs, which is confirmed in my series where no incestuous pregnancies have occurred, contrasts with the higher incidence reported in some published studies. For example, in the De Francis study, 11 percent of the girls became pregnant from the incest.[15] Maisch's study of German court cases revealed an 18 percent pregnancy rate,[16] and Tormes reported an intermediate percentage in her study of cases in Brooklyn.[17] Other studies over the past fifty years cited by Maisch report similar or even higher figures.

How can such a discrepancy be reconciled? The treatment program counselors are very familiar with their clients and would know about the occurrence of an incestuous pregnancy. This fact tends to validate their low figures. The published studies may be considered as cases which have not been treated, and in which the incest may have progressed further than the average case in the treatment programs. As will be seen, pregnancy is often a desperate measure taken to end the incest, and has been probably utilized more in the past, when the community was less sensitive to reacting to a possible incest situation and when treatment programs which allow families to work together were not available.

Reasons for Incestuous Pregnancies

The basic reason already given for teenage pregnancy operates also in incestuous pregnancies, i.e., to feel cared for by another person. There are many ways in which this can be expressed. If the girl has been told that her fertility is impaired, implying no one will ever love her for being able to create new life, she may test out her fertility as did the girl in Maisch's study who had been told by doctors she would never have children. The stepfather, who helped support the baby, was forgiven by the mother and all maintained residence while not letting the child know his paternity.[18] If the father has selected some but not other daughters for incest, the unchosen one may become pregnant to make him jealous of another man in an attempt to win him over from the other sisters.[19] This pregnancy can not be called strictly an incestuous pregnancy, just as many other pregnancies of girls also involved in incest cannot be considered incestuous pregnancies from the biological standpoint. However, insofar as the incestuous relationship motivates a pregnancy by another male, it could be considered as resulting from the incest in a psychological way. While none of my cases had incestuous pregnancies, most had pregnancies which could be said to relate to the incest, if for no other reason than to produce another person with whom the daughter could relate better than with the incestuous partner and other parent. Such pregnancies often serve as a replacement for the loss of the incestuous relationship, and her difficulty accepting the pregnancy may relate to her ambivalence about reestablishing the incestuous relationship.[20] Feeling basically inadequate and unacceptable, these girls hope that by bringing a baby along with them they will become more acceptable, especially to their mothers.[21] Perhaps the most obvious impact of the pregnancy is on the mother-daughter relationship. Here the pregnancy represents a desperate attempt to reestablish contact with the mother on the part of the incestuous daughter—a way of finally getting through to the mother what has been happening.

Incestuous Pregnancy—A Way to Stop the Incest

What does it take to stop incest? Tormes mentions several cases where the mother had seen or been explicitly told about the incest and ignored it until a pregnancy finally occasioned the reporting of the incest. Repeatedly seeing father in bed nude with daughter for two and a half years merely raised suspisions in one mother who finally reported the incest after a pregnancy occurred. In other cases the incestuous pregnancy was reported by another relative after the mother had been notified six years earlier or after the mother had reassured her four daughters that father was merely trying to show affection by manipulating their breasts and vaginas.[22]

Pregnancy of itself will not always prompt reporting, although it may be used as corroborative evidence when someone finally does report the incest. Fontana reported a family with four teenagers including three girls who had been involved in incest with the father and who were doing poorly in school. Mother had not reported the incest for fear of losing her husband and breaking up the family, although she was relieved not to be bothered by him sexually. The oldest daughter, who had his child at home, was 17 when she went to the police on behalf of her two sisters.[23] Gentry's experience in Appalachia, while acknowledging that "the pregnancy usually serves to stop the incest,"[24] notes some cases involving multiple incestuous pregnancies involving particularly isolated families. The psychological reaction of these girls involved is more pronounced. When pregnancy will not prompt the family to stop the incest, crazy behavior may be utilized to break the family incest pattern.

Lest exclusive responsibility for stopping the incest be attributed to the family, let us consider a case of Butler's where repeated complaints of pain in the genital area did not alert either mother or pediatrician to the incest involving a 10-year-old girl. With medical reassurance this mother "told her (daughter) to stop complaining about imaginary things and to get her mind off it." The daughter became pregnant at age 13. The mother said she still feels guilty that the daughter was trying to protect her against knowledge of the incest, adding "I should have been the one to protect her."[25] This case also highlights the estrangement between mother and daughter, in which pregnancy may be a way to focus attention on the mother-daughter relationship with the hope of improving it.

Incestuous Pregnancy—A Way to Unite Mother and Daughter

Incestuous daughters uniformly feel that their mothers were bad mothers and fear that they themselves will be bad mothers.[26] Giving their mothers another opportunity to raise a child may be considered a way to allow their mothers to become better mothers and, in turn, teach the daughters to be mothers. One mother in the Santa Clara program actually became the guardian of her daughter's baby and the parents are raising both the daughter and the baby of the daughter and father as their own. Members of another family in this program are similarly all living together. There were brief separations in both homes before moving back together, with the father leaving in the first family and the daughter in the second.[27] Families remaining intact after an incestuous pregnancy tend to experience more difficulties between the mother and daughter when the father is not the daughter's natural father. Jealousy and hostility marked the relationship between mother and daughter in five of Maisch's cases where a stepfather was involved.[28] Presumably it is more difficult for a stepdaughter to resume a role of daughter to a man who is not her natural father, and she still poses more of a threat as rival spouse than does a natural daughter.

In more cases, particularly involving stepfathers, there is a uniting of the mother and daughter after the stepfather leaves the family. There may be a common feeling expressed by both mother and daughter that the man has interfered with their relationship and each can relieve the other of feeling responsible by blaming the absent man.[29] At the San Francisco Emergency Sex Abuse program, a 14-year-old girl impregnated by her stepfather was invited back home after her younger sister protested and also left home rather than risk pregnancy by incest. Mother became assertive, said she did not want him around, and invited them both back home after he left. The family became involved in the treatment program.[30] A Denver social worker related the case of a man who had embezzled money and left the state with his 12-year-old daughter and settled in another state where he impregnated her and kept her fairly isolated. The pregnancy came to the attention of authorities, who arrested the man and sent the girl back to her mother. She wanted to give her mother the baby, possibly to make up for the loss of her husband and probably also as a peace offering since she had literally stolen her father away from her mother.[31]

Stepfathers may have a tenuous position in the family relationship, since the mother may feel a marital loyalty to the girl's natural father, and that she remarried mainly for economic reasons. One mother remarried when her daughter was 10 and left her new spouse and daughter alone while she went on an extended visit to her native country. On her return the daughter told her mother her menstrual periods had stopped, and mother, without any discussion, gave her pills to induce an abortion. When the pills did not work, the daughter tried unsuccessfully to abort by vigorous exercise in school. The daughter said that the mother finally "decided to keep the baby and raise it as her own son and a brother to the boy she had had with my stepfather the year before."[32] Even natural fathers can be sacrificed as mother, daughter, and child set up a home life which may reflect the increasing trend in single parent households. In a case recounted by Karen Cansino of the San Mateo County Incest Treatment Program, the mother and father were separated and planning divorce while the mother, daughter and child shared a home. Both women worked while the child attended a day care center.[33]

The single parent household involving a woman and children occurs also in incestuous homes where the pregnancy occurs by some non-related male. Here especially the maternal reeducation function of the pregnancy is evident. As one daughter who ran away from an incestuous home and became pregnant said of her mother and child, "She's become a traditional grandma, always bringing presents and games to my daughter. It gives me such pleasure to watch them together. My child is getting what neither of us ever had."[34] Another daughter, who returned home after father was sent to jail for incest, got pregnant by a next door neighbor. As most teenage mothers tend to be, this girl was passive and allowed her own mother to take care of the baby.[35] The baby is used as a substitute for the missing father and also as a reincarnation of both daughter and mother, giving them another opportunity to experience vicariously through the baby maternal warmth and protection which both feel they have lacked in the past.

Incestuous Pregnancies: A Way to Get Out of the House

Pregnancy may serve to stop the incest by creating a condition that takes the daughter out of the home. While the daughter may opt to go out on her own with her baby, as did one of the cases of Giarretto,[36] most daughters who leave are excluded by the parental pair as either delinquent, retarded, or mentally disturbed. Although the daughters may be escaping from the incest situation, being so labeled handicaps them in their future life, and particularly as a mother to their child. One 14-year-old girl considered retarded was sent to an institution for the retarded when she became pregnant by the father. Her sister, two years later and then 13 years old, was also involved in incest and had become a prostitute. A 15-year-old brother had likewise been sent away from the family, since the mother was determined to stay with the father regardless of his behavior and the loss of their children. Although the mother and younger 13-year-old daughter have been sporadically involved in therapy, the father has not. A 6-year-old daughter remains in the home.[37]

In another case related by Myers, a woman seen long after the incestuous pregnancy had been labeled crazy and institutionalized for several years while her parents raised her son, who is now 18. This woman is now married with two other children.[38] For a girl who had been doing poorly at school since age 9, involved in thefts and running away from home since age 12, and sexually involved with her father and other boys from age 15 to 19, an incestuous pregnancy prompted her father to eject her from the house. Her delinquency stopped when she took care of her baby and married at age 20.[39]

In all these cases, leaving home after the incestuous pregnancy served at least to stop the incest. Leaving home too early, however, can lead a girl to recreate the home situation and gives her a chance to change it on the one hand but may impede individual development on the other. A girl who had coital relations with her father since age 9 became pregnant by a boy she met in high school. She said:

> [It] wasn't different than with my father. It was all
> pretty quick, and he didn't even look at me the
> whole time. But I got pregnant. Daddy and Mother
> said I had brought disgrace on the family and had
> to get out.

Since incest was considered normal in her family, whereas illegitimate pregnancy was a disgrace, this girl found herself indulging in some "normal" behavior with her 8-month-old baby, "touching him on his private parts, and (in her words) I got scared that I was going to do the same thing to him that Daddy had done to me." While she never let herself do that again, she confessed, "that was the start of my using drugs (which was a way to) withdraw so nobody (would) know how awful I was."[40]

Leaving home prematurely may not end the incest, but serve to carry it on to another generation. One woman had a son by her father, prompting her to stop the incest and leave home. With her knowledge, her son eventually became involved in an incestuous relationship with his 5-year-old cousin for whom he babysat.[41] In all of these cases, the pregnancy served as a way to end the current incest without prompting much change in the attitudes of family members. Shifts in the relationships occurred, usually with father or daughter leaving the home situation, reinforcing the assumption that mother and daughter were rivals and could not tolerate each other's presence around the father. Incestuous pregnancy merely duplicates the problem by adding to the family another person who usually substitutes for the loss of another family member. The mode of incestuous family relations remains the same unless all members change their attitude and mode of behavior. Nor does the pregnancy itself stop the incest necessarily, as indicated by a case in San Mateo County of a retarded girl who remained with her father after the mother left the home when the daughter became pregnant by the father. In spite of efforts made to urge her to procure an abortion, she did not have one and remained with her father expecting their baby.[42]

Incestous Pregnancy: Effect of the Pregnancy on Daughter and Child

We have seen that the child born from an incestuous union may live to perpetuate the incest pattern if no efforts are made at improving the family relationships. Furthermore, we have reviewed some reasons for the occurrence of incestuous pregnancies which serve in various ways to stop the immediate incestuous pattern. The following example of how a daughter may utilize pregnancy to stop the incest is afforded by Fontana, who tells of an 11-year-old girl who had coital relations with her father on six occasions and was warned by her father, "Your mother will never believe you." When she was found to be 26 weeks pregnant she could prove her father wrong in perhaps the most dramatic way. Yet she received little support from her mother, delivered a stillborn child, and was sent to an institution where she appeared contented and docile for a while and then turned increasingly hostile and obstreperous.[43] Denied the protective love of her parents and the fruit of her sexual activity, her reaction of bitter resentment is understandable. Her baby may have suffered from genetic defects, which have been found in one study to lead to death or major birth defects in 6 of 18 incestuously-conceived pregnancies.[44] However, such a pregnancy outcome is uncommon and depends on the genetic quality of the family.

In contrast with the experience related by Myers of children conceived from rape situations in which mothers displaced their hatred from the rapist and themselves onto the child,[45] incestuous pregnancies may be a positive experience for the girl, depending on the reaction of those around her. The sexual partner provides an important role in determining the girl's reaction and the outcome of the pregnancy. Only 3 of Maisch's 13 cases of incestuous pregnancies had negative feelings toward the father, derived from his insistence she get an abortion or deny his paternity. Yet even some of the girls whose fathers pressed for rejecting the consequences of their sexual activity (i.e., abortion) were positively inclined toward them. Most of Maisch's sample of 13 were positively inclined toward their partner during the pregnancy, including 3 who were passionately in love with their fathers. Problems in accepting the pregnancy and birth of the child seemed related more to the negative reaction of friends and other relatives and to tensions which developed between the parents or between mother and daughter as a result of the pregnancy. Maisch concludes from his evaluation of this series of pregnancies that, "the damage is less physical . . . than psychological as a result of the grave nature of the offense and the discriminating reactions of people around her."[46]

Incestuous Pregnancy: Adoption as an Option

What can be the outcome of a pregnancy conceived with one's father? This question could be rephrased in the following manner: How can an incestuous pregnancy serve to stop the incest pattern with its devastating effect on the life of the daughter? Or more specifically, can the incestuous pregnancy help the girl acknowledge her incestuous tie to her father and then give up the baby? Clearly, babies conceived from incestuous unions are not wanted for themselves but rather are wanted to serve the needs of the family, which, in most cases, includes the need to stop the incest activity. Or more precisely, the pregnancies may be wanted to stop the incest but the babies may be not needed or wanted at all for themselves. Since a teenage girl invariably feels unwanted herself in a family when she conceives a child, and since an incestuous daughter is not being wanted as a daughter but rather as a sexual plaything, any move to assure her that she is wanted as a daughter will serve to prevent teenage pregnancy.

There is always a question in a girl's mind as she contemplates her incestuously conceived baby whether her parents want her as a daughter or rather want her for what she can do to provide them with a better daughter. The best way to resolve this question in her favor is for all concerned to give up the baby. Then, and only then, will she be able to accept her role as daughter and wait for a more auspicious occasion to become a parent, with someone she can share her life with forever. Adopted out to parents ready to raise a child as their own, her baby can enjoy the natural benefit of regarding himself as the fruit of his parents' creative love, while avoiding the confusion of relating to parents, grandparents, and siblings interchangeably as he would experience in the incestuous family. To avoid the confusion of considering his grandfather as his father, his mother as his sister, and his grandmother as his mother, there would be a tendency to want to eliminate people to avoid such confusion, a situation which often occurs in the incestuous family where father or daughter are usually extruded from the family. Then there would be the quest for one's parents, for uniting one's parents, which is the dream of every child and upon which his future security is based.

If there was ever a clear indication for adoption as an option to pregnancy outcome, it is in the case of the incestuous pregnancy. The fact that pregnancy has occurred indicates that other avenues of stopping the incest have been closed. To improve family relations such that an incestuously conceived child can adequately relate to all his relatives is nearly impossible by nature of the confused interelationships, but it is even more difficult for families who have resorted to pregnancy to alter the incest pattern. The success of the new incest treatment programs, which claim very high percentages of maintaining the family intact and no recidivism of incestuous behavior, is based mainly on families that have not resorted to incestuous pregnancies.[47] The argument that giving up one's child is psychologically damaging must be weighed against the conditions under which the child was conceived. A more appropriate question would be, "Is it more damaging to care for a child which presents a constant reminder that one has usurped the prerogative of one's mother and refused to be a child oneself?"

> Only after having the child adopted can there be some assurance that this new life will not simply become part of the incestuous family affair. The family can be consoled by the knowledge that they have broken their incestuous pattern by giving life to the world rather than keeping it to themselves.

The need for a child to fulfill oneself or complete a relationship with another is the basis for poor parenting and child abuse. Perhaps such a need was felt, according to Barbara Myers, by a girl who had ulcerative colitis, became incestuously pregnant, gave her child up for adoption, and got cancer and died. She appeared to have given up her will to live after having her baby adopted.[48] As harsh as it may seem, babies are not supposed to keep their parents alive. On the contrary, parents, by participating in the creative act in forming new life, pledge to give up their life so that their child may have more abundant life.

II. Life-taking: Abortion

Historical Review of Abortions for Incest

Giving life for life and taking life for life are social principles that have been codified in law since the earliest Judaic formulations. Exodus 21:22-3 calls for the death of a man who causes a woman to abort, "Thou shalt give life for life." Judaic preoccupation with the stage of development is also evident, as Philo, the Jewish philosopher of Alexandria, declared that the attacker must die if the lost child was "shaped and all the limbs had their proper qualities (which then defined) a human being."[49] While incest itself was considered a capital crime (Leviticus 20:10-20), as has been mentioned, the children conceived from incestuous relations were not killed; they were socially restricted from marriage with anyone except others incestuously conceived, thereby effectively ending their life as social progenitors but not ending their individual lives. Today, dooming a person to an unmarried or childless state is often considered a boon,[50] so the child conceived of incest escapes the Jewish solution of "eye for an eye," especially since he will be sufficiently formed upon the discovery to be considered a human being.

Pagan civilization was much harsher to incestuous unborn babies, with the Greek philosopher Plato recommending abortion for incestuous pregnancies in his *Republic*,[51] and Roman law allowing infanticide as well as abortion.[52] Christian influence protected the life of the child but has not been effective in English and American law, which has always allowed the taking of the unborn child's life to preserve that of the mother.[53] Since this maternal protection has been interpreted in the physical sense until recently,[54] incest has become a separate consideration which will be dealt with later under indications for abortion.

A look at some primitive societies bears out the pagan experience where abortion has been widely practiced for incest with various rationalizations. The incestuous child is seen as a bad omen among several tribes where the anonymity of adoption is not possible. Thus the Zulus believe that such children, though normal at first, are later turned into monsters by the angry "spirits of the elders." The Navaho believe the live birth of an incestuous child will bring catastrophe to the whole tribe.[55] The Gunantuna require abortion of incestuous children and all illegitimate children, according to Devereux in his *Study of Abortion in Primitive Societies*. As an example of the compounded abuse of incest and abortion he tells of "a Sedang father, who both impregnated and aborted his daughter, and then palmed her off on an unsuspecting husband, pretending that she had cohabited with other men." Too ashamed to admit either the incest or the abortion, "the daughter herself, when she was asked about the blood on the lower part of her body, explained that she had been bitten by leeches."[56] Devereux concludes with a hypothesis that

> compulsory abortion, especially of the more or less public and legal kind, suggests that the fetus is unconsciously believed to be, or is in fact, the child of a socially improper father, and that, on further analysis, one may tentatively assume that this improper impregnator is fantasied to be the man's or, occasionally the woman's father (or at least father surrogate or father image).[57]

Primitive societies, therefore, consider abortions as a way to purify the society of ill-conceived children whose prototype is the child of incest. For societies like the Mohave who have such a strong taboo on incest as to self-destruct the entire incestuous family, both incestuous pregnancy and abortion are reportedly rare. Abortion in such a society is equally frowned upon, as evidenced by the fact that crippled babies raise suspicion that the mother had tried to abort the baby.[58]

Incidence of Incestuous Abortions

Studies of incestuous pregnancies have invariably revealed that more pregnancies are allowed to go to term than are aborted.[59] Even when the incestuous fathers pressed for abortion, there was usually a resistance to abort noted in Maisch's study where, despite such pressure from nearly half the fathers, only a quarter of the daughters actually aborted.[60] Giarretto reports a similar incidence of abortions among the five pregnancies in his group.[61] While the argument may be made that in Germany ten years ago abortion may not have been an easily obtainable option for Maisch's cases, there can be no such argument made for the San Francisco Bay area, where the passage of the California Therapeutic Abortion Act of 1967, the U.S. Supreme Court decisions of 1973 (*Roe* v. *Wade* and *Doe* v. *Bolton*), and the activity of Planned Parenthood have led "75 percent of those (teenagers) who are pregnant (to) elect abortion."[62] Even before the Supreme Court decisions and the passage of a California law in 1975 that teenagers could obtain abortions without parental consent,[63] Planned

Parenthood of San Francisco was turning away those teens who wished to continue their pregnancy, so that ultimately 95 percent of their clients "elected abortion."[64]

In the early 1970s, California was one of only a few states to specifically and "clearly authorize abortion in the case of incest."[65] Since California was among the first states to allow easy access to abortion, there was an early attempt required by law to justify the abortions based on the specified indications.[66] During the first half of 1968, 91 percent of the 2,324 applications for abortion were granted. Five percent were done for the physical health of the mother, 7 percent for rape, and 88 percent for the mental health of the mother. Adding these percentages yields 100 percent. Where were the abortions for incest? They comprised a mere 0.3 percent and represent all of the incestuous pregnancies presented for abortion at the time, for none of the six incest cases were denied abortion, whereas the refusal rate was highest for rape, physical health, and mental health in that order.[67] In spite of the attempts of the California Abortion Act of 1967 and its later amended version to be precise about criteria, the California Supreme Court struck them down as too vague just two months before the U.S. Supreme Court decisions of 1973. Since the criteria were too vague, the "requirements for approval by medical committees and for involvement of district attorneys and courts in cases of pregnancy resulting from rape or incest are (were) invalidated also."[68] There is little indication that the current federal and state legislative restrictions on abortion for incest are any less vague, even for a state which has had a previous experience reporting abortions for incest.[69]

One might conclude that Planned Parenthood's favoring abortion as an option would result in the abortion of most incestuous pregnancies, but this has not proven true. In the Washington state incest program, where the director is also on the board of directors of Planned Parenthood and refers all clients to Planned Parenthood, there are also fewer abortions than live births. A surprising finding to director Peter Coleman is the relatively low frequency of pregnancies among incestuous daughters he knows are genitally active. Even more significant is the fact that there have been no pregnancies from the incest *per se*. The few pregnancies which have occurred have been the result of liaisons with boyfriends, so that the even fewer abortions do not represent incestuous pregnancies, strictly speaking.[70]

Incestuous Pregnancy as an Indication for Abortion

England has sidestepped the question of rape and incest indications in its 1967 Abortion Act and, like most other countries allowing abortion, the law provides broad enough indications so as not to focus on such specific problems.[71] However, for over a decade the United States has been modeling its laws after the recommendations of the American Law Institute, which specifically mentions rape and incest under what has been generally considered humanitarian indications.[72] "Although these so-called 'humanitarian' indications are often enumerated separately in the laws, they are frequently considered psychiatric indications in the medical literature."[73] Anderson in an article entitled, "Psychiatric Indications for the Termination of Pregnancy," refers to girls with incestuous pregnancies not being ready for a child and the social isolation brought by caring for the child and, if the child is put up for adoption, the guilt later from giving up the child.[74] Sloane admits in the *New England Journal of Medicine* that "the psychological effect of a continued pregnancy resulting from rape or incest does not seem to have been much studied," but concludes that "most would agree that it is psychologically undesirable."[75]

The issue of indications for abortion was discussed thoroughly twenty-three years ago at a Planned Parenthood conference that led to the publishing of a comprehensive scientific work promoting easy access to abortion. At that conference, Dr. Mary Calderone posed the question, "But is it not true that fundamentally most therapeutic abortions are actually being granted because of socio-economic and humanitarian reasons that are masked as psychiatric or other medical reasons?"[76] After several physicians attempted to justify abortion for the health of the family, including the health of mother, children, and husband, Dr. Laidlow added that such health considerations beg the issue, and Dr. Calderone concluded that medical, including psychiatric, indications represented a "dishonest expediency." Present was Dr. Theodore Lidz, a psychiatrist world famous for his concepts of pathological family relationships, "marital schism" and "marital skew," who had said in an earlier conference he was "concerned about the liberalizing of abortion laws on pseudo-medical grounds." "This would place psychiatrists," he said, "in the uncomfortable, if not untenable, position of being expected to make decisions they cannot honestly make." He supported with examples his contention that "the question of the need for abortion is often broached without ample consideration of psychotherapy as an alternative."[77] Nevertheless, the conference concluded with recommending that the American Law Institute's indications be accepted to justify more abortions, "since with the improvement of modern medicine it rarely becomes necessary to perform an abortion to save life."[78]

Since these pioneer conferences over twenty years ago, psychiatrists have generally compromised or prostituted themselves and their profession despite Dr. Lidz's warning, such that hospital committees were formed to reduce the excessive number of psychiatric medications.[79] In another pro-abortion scientific conference fifteen years after the first, Dr. Laidlow echoed Dr. Eisenberg, who admitted that "in many cases we must go out on a limb to find some indication which fits in with existing laws." He averred that, "we can always say that the patient is depressed and that if her pregnancy continues, this depression may become severe and even assume suicidal proportions."[80] Disregarded in this scientific rationale of the end justifying the means was data proving not only that pregnant women are much less likely to commit suicide than non-pregnant women,[81] but also that those who have actually threatened suicide do not kill themselves when denied an abortion.[82]

Although there are no specific studies of the effects of incestuous pregnancies on the women who carry to term, Simon writing in 1971 on the "Psychological and Emotional Indications for Therapeutic Abortion," considered incest as one of the four "specific areas in which psychiatric indication for abortion can be stated with some clarity." How can such a supposedly scientific judgment be made without any scientific evidence? Simon answers this question by an appeal to authority, for he has "not been able to discover any scientific voices raised in support of encouraging maintenance of pregnancies from incestuous unions." Thus, there is a psychiatric indication for abortion for incestuous pregnancies simply because no psychiatrist has said there shouldn't be. Realizing the weakness of an exclusive negative appeal to authority, Sloane adds parenthetically that it is "clear the genetic outcome is depressing in such unions," and refers to the two small studies where less than 50 percent of the offspring were of normal intelligence. Yet in his conclusion that "these are clearly good reasons to recommend termination" for incestuous pregnancies, Simon excludes genetic outcome from his psychiatric consideration.[83]

The one argument used by psychiatrists with any shred of evidence to support it has been branded a myth by one incest worker who cites a small study of several university students who were conceived of father-daughter unions. He deplores the fact that "many professionals have decided in advance that the child of the union should be aborted," considering it "unfair to the child and its parents." He puts the matter in the hands of a geneticist rather than a psychiatrist, whom he expects the parents to consult before a decision to abort is made.[84] The psychiatric basis for terminating the life of an unborn baby incestuously conceived has absolutely no scientific merit and derives from a blind adherence to a legal formulation espoused by abortion promoters, now including organized psychiatry.[85] Psychiatrists have allowed themselves to be used as agents of social control, although they are the last group to acknowledge this function publicly. Social policy statements made by others, that society has no duty to protect offspring from an incestuous union,[86] will always need to be implemented by respectable social agents now given the power to protect or destroy life for the social welfare.

Implementation of Abortion for Incestuous Pregnancy

For those who have worked so hard to overcome impediments to easy access to legal abortion and who have become accustomed to obtaining abortions without any indication (i.e., without a psychiatrist, without a medical committee, without a police report, without a compulsory treatment program for an indefinite period) returning to incest as an indication for abortions can only be seen as a giant step backward. Most states either do not have a mechanism for recording such incestuous pregnancies and abortions or have abandoned it since the Supreme Court decisions of 1973. There is little, if any, evidence that the restrictions of public funding of abortion by the Congress in 1977 has produced any statistics on incestuous abortions.[87] Given the sharp reduction in federally funded abortions, which have been cut by 99 percent,[88] and the low incidence of reported incestuous pregnancies, one would expect that the federal government would not bother with the elaborate mechanism needed to determine the few, if any, incestuous pregnancies presented for funded abortion. The states that have continued funding abortions with state money have not required incest as a criterion or, if they have, have no mechanism for adequately reporting abortions for incest.[89] Nor can they seriously be expected to develop a reporting mechanism for such an indication, which has already served as an emotional argument for easy access to abortion, has been found wanting in scientific validity, has hardly ever been used when there are any other indications which could cover the same situation, and is probably unenforceable.

Law enforcement experts have argued that the necessary investigation required to establish an incestuous pregnancy would overburden their agencies, especially if false reports were made[90] and subsequently had to be investigated for fraud.[91] The father could claim in defense that another man is the father of the baby in order to escape a jail sentence.[92] Since paternity cannot be proven sufficiently by medical science,[93] this would become a standard defense and would disqualify a girl incestuously impregnated from obtaining a legal abortion. The family already disrupted by incest would be further divided by such legal intervention. The girl, already estranged from her mother by nature of the incest, will be legally estranged from her father to whom she has turned for affection, thereby leaving her isolated. As the wheels of justice grind exceedingly slowly, and since incestuous pregnancies are usually uncovered after the first trimester, the late abortions will further burden the girl with physical complications most other aborters are spared. Despite some cavalier reports of midtrimester abortions being "done safely,"[94] studies of abortion complications consistently show a relatively high complication rate in second and third trimester abortions.[95]

The controversy over abortion indications, swept away for several years by the Supreme Court decisions of 1973, has been rekindled by the ongoing debate over public funding of abortion. Recognized as a "dishonest expediency" by pro-abortion physicians over twenty years ago with no medical or psychiatric evidence to support abortion as a treatment for any indication, including incest, the flames may be fanned anew to protect what has become more a public right than a legal option. Sarvis sums up the issue clearly:

> Debates about determining the validity of rape and incest indications for abortion and whether abortion is the "answer" for women who become pregnant as a result of rape or incest seem rather absurd when one considers the infinitesimal number of abortions performed for rape or incest, and the enormous amount of red tape necessary to obtain an abortion for these humanitarian indications.[96]

A pro-abortion feminist handbook published in 1969 and rendered obsolete by the 1973 Supreme Court decisions may come back into vogue with the following advice to abortion seekers:

> If rape and incest aren't your speed,
> For abortion care, a psychosis you need.
> In order to prove you're as mad as a hatter,
> Let's practice a little psychiatrist chatter.[97]

Psychological Setting for Abortion of an Incestuous Pregnancy

Since abortions of incestuous pregnancies are even rarer than incestuous pregnancies, there is little documented evidence about the reaction of the girl to such an abortion. A key element in the response to the abortion compares with the response to the incest itself, and that is denial of the responsibility for the act. There are few human activities that appear more prone to promote denial of responsibility than incest and abortion. The consequences of such denial of the incest are described elsewhere by this author in terms of promiscuity, homosexuality, prostitution, drug and alcohol abuse, obesity, school failure, self-mutilation and suicide, all serving to protect the girl from acknowledging responsibility for her sexual feelings and incestuous acts. Pregnancy occurs when the girl has elicited the aid of another person, her unborn child, to help her acknowledge the incest and get out of the incest situation.

While pregnancy reveals the possibility of incest, abortion perpetuates the denial of responsibility for incest. In no other situation involving pregnancy is abortion more clearly revealed as an assault on a woman than in incestuous pregnancies, where the father forces an abortion and even performs it himself on his daughter as occurred in two of Maisch's three abortion cases and at least one of Tormes' cases. Another daughter in Maisch's study refused her father's suggestion for an abortion so as not to destroy the evidence against her father, who had denied the incest and accused her of having coital relations with other men. Later she had considered that an abortion might permanently damage her health and prevent her from having children later on,[98] thereby confirming her resolution to acknowledge the incest while absolving herself of responsibility for it.

As reported by three women professionals in the 1974 meeting of the American Psychiatric Association "each woman [after abortion] later stressed the feeling that the decision was not really her own."[99] More recently Nancy Kaltrieder of the University of California Medical Center in San Francisco cited in a study reported at a local psychiatric meeting the denial of responsibility for the abortion as a predominant feature in the woman's response to the abortion. The women responded by comments such as "it was out of my hands—like a dream" or "I closed my eyes—I don't want to relate to it as a potential living being." Kaltreider considers this denial beneficial and advocates the dilatation and extraction procedure which involves general anesthesia so that the women can actually perpetuate the delusion that the abortion was a dream.[100]

When a girl will not accept responsibility for her incestuous sexual activity, even when pregnancy ensues, and she does not develop the various post-incestuous symptomatology and the family breaks up, there is greater likelihood that abortion will be employed. In a case of Barbara Myers, a 15-year-old aborted after her mother left her father and went to another town. The girl did away with her father's baby just as her mother had done away with her father. This girl has been undergoing psychotherapy for a psychological reaction after the abortion.[101]

Coleman's two cases of abortion resulted not from the incestuous union but in close proximity to it. In one, the girl was a passive participant as parents and Planned Parenthood arranged for the abortion. The other resisted going to Planned Parenthood, claiming she wanted to be a "virgin for life"; but after becoming pregnant by her fiance she went to Planned Parenthood and procured an abortion and subsequently married. She now boasts after four months of marriage that she is "thinking," which to her means not getting pregnant.[102] One wonders what marriage means to this girl who has killed the fruit of the sexual union with her husband, and whose "thinking" requires her not to get pregnant. How can she think to plan a pregnancy? Will a pregnancy ever survive in such a relationship? Will such a relationship survive? Such questions can only be answered by longitudinal research on incestuous pregnancies and abortions.

Research studies already done on young girls who abort can be applied to some degree to incestuous daughters. Rosenthal's study revealed that the girls' sexual activity reflected "parental wishes,"[103] which would suggest in an incest situation that the girl is being used for her sexual services by the parents, who then reap the fruit of her womb and either enjoy it or destroy it. A study by Susan Fishman, presented at an annual meeting of the American Public Health Association, compared girls who delivered with those who aborted, and found that the aborters had lower self-esteem and poorer relations with their mothers. "Moreover, the deliverers indicated a purposeful attempt to become pregnant and happiness with the event."[104] The desire for the pregnancy may be revealed years later—Barbara Myers has found women saying they had wished for a pregnancy to stop the incest, but the fear of pregnancy had overcome the wish in most. If pregnancy is a way out of the incest, and abortion is a way out of the pregnancy, then the purpose of the pregnancy is ill-served by the abortion. As already noted, one girl refused an abortion because she wanted to maintain evidence to support her claim of incest. She saw abortion being used in the service of denying the incest and wanted to acknowledge the incest and its consequences, at least as far as the pregnancy was concerned.

How the abortion can cover up the feelings of the girl or misdirect them is exemplified by the case of a 13-year-old girl whose father was removed from the home and for whom a date was set for an abortion. The girl had "not shown any emotion" until she was told she would have to wait three weeks for a second trimester abortion. The counselor used this time to talk about the girl's feelings. One wonders whether her feelings would ever have been discussed had the delay not occurred. Following the abortion the mother and daughter expressed anger at the father for having disrupted their lives and for having victimized the daughter. There was no mention of how the abortion itself might have been distressing and how they were victimizing the unborn child. Their anger at the father could well have been displaced anger at themselves and the abortion counselor for killing the child.[105]

As with all abortion counseling there is a mutual avoidance of angry feelings between counselor and client. The hidden message goes something like this: "Don't blame me and I won't blame you and we'll both blame that awful man who did this thing to me (you)." Abortion counselors are biased against the idea of "a young teenager carrying a child to term" and "refuse to admit that having a child might be a healthier experience for a woman who would go through life blaming herself for the abortion that 'killed her baby.' " So stated Cynthia Martin who wrote a doctoral dissertation on the psychology of abortion and said she "knew of no agency in California that (she) could recommend wholeheartedly for counseling." She added that "to be an abortion counselor you must also be an adoption counselor and know how to keep the baby (and) about marriage." She concluded that "I think abortion is a lousy method of birth control—psychologically, physically, and socially"; also, that "if we talked more openly about the psychological and physical hazards involved in abortion, there might be fewer of them."[106]

Yet abortion counselors will fight to preserve their incestuous patients, who more than any other clients seem to make their deadly job worthwhile. Magda Denes tells the touching story of Debbie, 12 years old and six months pregnant by her uncle who was her stepfather for 10 years and who had been taken away to jail. Denes wrote of her experience in this abortion clinic that,

> Thanks to Debbie, the seventh floor experiences a spirit of solidarity bordering on joy. The belief that the work done here is truly in the service of humankind is manifest again in the swollen-bellied body of this little girl, whom everyone in concerted effort wants to spare and comfort. There is a live child on this floor whose future people are hard at work to save.

The inexorable life-boat ethic charts the waters in this abortion clinic as it does everywhere—a better life is used as an excuse for causing death. Both Debbie and the staff miss the boat in understanding her tears.

"What hurts Debbie?" Denes asks, and Debbie replies:

> I don't want him to be in jail, where they put him. I
> love my uncle. He was like a father to me. We
> played games. It was wrong, but I miss my uncle.

Could Debbie be crying also because she misses her baby?
She will not be able to explore this at the abortion clinic where the
attendants "give her candy" and call her "little Debbie," denying
that she is a mother and has killed her child with their help.[107] The
voices of two well-known psychiatrists, Drs. Theodore Lidz and
Lawrence Kolb are unheard in abortion clinics today as they re-
called in 1955

> instances in which women were allowed to talk
> themselves out of having an abortion, although we
> would have been willing to recommend one
> because we had found some degree of depression
> present. In discussing the general circumstances,
> the women, now that they saw it in a different light,
> decided to have the child. They are among the
> most grateful patients we have had, and although
> my [Dr. Lidz's] contact with them was limited to
> two or three interviews, when I see one of them she
> reminds me that this was a very important factor in
> her life.[108]

Various Consequences Illustrated by Case Histories

Dr. Lidz also enumerated several attitudes he had found resulting from abortions procured early in a woman's life. These
consequences he shared with Dr. Iago Galdston, who also claimed
that "any abortion is likely to have serious traumatic sequelae."[109]

1. Guilt at doing away with the baby

Case No. 11 is that of a 22-year-old single woman with a 4-
year-old son. She lives with her mother with whom she is very
angry. No mention of the incest with her father, which occurred
from age 5 to 13, was made in a meeting with her mother just
prior to the abortion, although the incest is the source of her anger
at her mother. She initially presented difficulties relating to her
boyfriend and claimed the incest had made it impossible for her
to get close to a man. She had asked her son if he wanted the
baby she was carrying and he had said yes. Nevertheless, she obtained an abortion. Subsequently, she reported frightening homi-
cidal thoughts toward her mother and son, and actually envisioned
blood coming out of her son. She regretted the abortion, about

which she had nightmares and for which she felt like killing herself, and presented herself to a hospital for self-protection.

As with this and the subsequent cases to be cited, the abortion did not involve an incestuous pregnancy strictly speaking, but
did involve women who had been involved in incest. The characteristic feature of these women as opposed to other women involved in incest who did not abort is the more pronounced feeling
of rejection by the mother and an inability to confront the mother
with their feelings regarding the incest. This case, while exemplify-
ing the guilt at having the abortion, also demonstrates how difficult it is for an aborter simply to acknowledge her responsibility
for the abortion and be done with it. Her unwillingness to do this
results in the abortion, which serves as a dramatic replay in which
she identifies with her mother who had given her up to father, and
she identifies her son with the unborn baby she killed. Her wish to
commit suicide was a way of punishing herself for the act she re-
lived whereby she saw blood coming out of her son. This woman
was seen on three occasions prior to the abortion and has not kept
subsequent appointments, and occasionally calls in distress.

2. Loss of self-esteem at being willing to forego the baby in order
to have whatever else it is that the woman desires in life, whatever it may be.

Case No. 5 had aborted her third pregnancy after giving up
her first two children for foster care. She had enjoyed arousing her
father in the bathtub as a child, justifying her behavior by her impression that her mother deprived him sexually. Mother and
grandmother had poisoned him, and she felt her mother not only
rejected her but wanted her to get another abortion when she became pregnant a fourth time. She had obtained the abortion after
her fiance had broken off plans for the wedding; after the abortion
she had asked "Where is my baby?" She felt inferior to her sister,
who was married, and inadequate to pursue schooling and an
occupation. Her life was preoccupied with sexual exploits, including recent coital relations with her half-brother. Her subsequent
pregnancy by yet another man was a second chance offered to her
boyfriend to marry her and a way to avoid further promiscuity,
which he had claimed turned him off to the marriage earlier. At
last contact she had moved in with her boyfriend and was planning to deliver the baby. Since he had tried at the last minute to
stop her from having an abortion and had said, "You killed my
baby," she wanted to avoid further guilt. She had aborted mainly
because the baby was not his and had feared he would definitely
break off their relationship had he seen the baby.

3. Fear of retaliation.

Case No. 12 had always had a strained relationship with her mother, who felt that her husband loved the daughter more than her. She had been conceived on a day when mother gave in to pacify her drunk, abusive husband. Years later, the mother discovered father and her now 9-year-old daughter sleeping nude one night, and had exposed them to her son, age 15, who subsequently has been under psychiatric care. Mother had been abandoned by her mother when she was 12, and had tried to care for her father who raised the seven children. She had divorced her husband, who was now still writing love letters to her daughter. The daughter objected to mother telling others about her sexual exploits and venereal disease. Mother finally moved away with another younger daughter, leaving her to roam the streets as a 15-year-old runaway. The daughter's biggest fear was being restricted, whether at home or in an institution. When she became pregnant and procured an abortion it was to avoid having to go to a girl's residence. Maintaining her freedom allowed her to keep in touch with her alcoholic father. Maintaining her pregnancy-free status neutralized the incestuous overtones of this relationship, as did her promiscuity. She now lives in constant fear of being reported to the police by her mother and being sent to an institution.

4. Fear of what she had done to herself; this type of woman might forfeit marriage, thinking she was sterile or try over again to become pregnant before marriage.

Case No. 5 exemplifies this phenonemon in her repeat pregnancy and guilt over aborting her last pregnancy. In addition, case No. 13, a 30-year-old woman with a son, was about to have an abortion, as she felt she and her husband would not long be together. They were returning to her home town where her parents lived. As a child her father had teased her in the mornings, pulling the sheet off her bed and arousing her. As an adult he has encouraged her to maintain a relationship with an old lesbian friend even after her marriage, which was unstable. After the abortion, she anticipated a future living arrangement where she would be close to her father while living with her girlfriend. She feared social stigma if she were to raise a second child without a father. Although she was not seen after the abortion, one possible reaction could be a feeling that the abortion had shut off a possible fertile future with a man should she wish to resume her marital relationship after killing her husband's baby. Furthermore, in some way she was modeling herself after her husband's daughter by a previous marriage. The 17-year-old daughter had recently undergone an abortion. Possibly she was relating to her husband as a daughter since there was only a 13-year difference in their ages. Her lesbian affair, which was promoted by her father, was meant to be a sterile one so as to avoid her becoming too involved with another man. The abortion was an indication of her inability to relate in a fruitful way with a man, a consequence of the incest compounded by the abortion.

5. Resentment toward the father (of the baby). If he insisted on the abortion she resents him for not making it possible for her to have the baby. He gets what he wants while she must degrade herself to have an abortion. Even if she does not want marriage she will still not want to have intercourse with him.

6. Delayed reaction in middle age with the self-derogation of involutional melancholia.

7. A feeling of inferiority in incurring the label "mentally ill and cannot have this baby."

8. The non-supportive setting of an abortion clinic may be so degrading that she will renounce sexual activity to avoid another abortion and (this may) lead to marital difficulties.

Case No. 3 best exemplifies these last four psychological reactions to an abortion in a woman who was involved in incest. Like the other cases, she felt rejection by her mother and was closer to her father. The incest occurred between her second husband and her daughter by her first husband, who had urged her to have an abortion as a condition for marriage. She resented her first husband for not making it possible to have the baby and for leaving her alone for several days to suffer the physical sequelae of pain, fever, and hemorrhage. She has finally admitted feeling estranged from her daughter who resented her divorcing her father. She also recognizes that she was not physically affectionate with her daughter and expected her second husband to be more demonstrative with the daughter, thereby setting up the incest situation. After a mental breakdown in her early forties treated with electroshock, she has retained a sense of inferiority, marked by a need to seek approval from others and a tendency to give herself to men indiscriminately and then resent their lack of involvement with her. She could not say no to her first fiance's desire for her to abort nor could she say no to her second husband's sexual advances or insistence she work full time. Killing her baby and undergoing a mental breakdown, which still leaves her disabled, were alternatives to asserting herself. Instead of saying "I won't abort or work to get married or stay married," she has adopted the inadequate stance of "I must do this or no one will have me." Then, presumably, the choice is not hers, but an action forced upon her. To adopt such an irresponsible position indicates the woman is not in control of her life and therefore can not protect the life of the child within her and is unable to prevent him from getting there in the first place.

The unwillingness to accept responsibility for the abortion is a corollary to the unwillingness to accept responsibility for the incest. The defective self-image one must maintain to preserve this sense of irresponsibility translates into the various psychological attitudes and behaviors already mentioned, all of which are based on a refusal to accept the consequences of one's acts, which is otherwise considered denial.

The Physician's Abdication of Responsibility: Denial of a Viable Alternative

Physicians have departed from the Hippocratic oath, which prohibits death-dealing, with special emphasis on aiding a woman to procure an abortion. Medicine itself has altered its ethical stance for life.

> [While] there are no medical indications for abortion, there are virtually no medical contraindications against abortion. [This view] places the doctor in the role of a technician, simply wielding the curette, but not solely at the insistence of the patient. [Moreover, he should humbly accept his new role.] This may be humiliating to him. But it is his unavoidable plight if we are to grant women their inherent right to abortion.

So goes the pro-abortion logic expressed in a professional conference nearly ten years ago.[110] A professor of obstetrics and gynecology at this conference pleaded for someone to come up with a "new term that would do for this business what 'family planning' has done for birth control." "If we could call this something more acceptable than abortion," he said, "we would get the public attitude to change a little faster."[111]

But some doctors won't go along completely with the white-wash of abortion. They may back out of the business, as Bernard Nathanson did after realizing he had killed 60,000 babies.[112] He may restrict the number or type of abortion he does each day, claiming that "Killing a baby is not the way I want to see myself," or that he "doesn't want others to call [him] the Killer."[113] Although a rare incestuously pregnant Debbie may come along, the sheer number of dead babies affects all those working in an abortion mill. In her interviews with the staff, Denes writes that, "The word 'murder' surfaces again and again, and it sticks on the tongue like a searing coal of fire that one knows will do further damage whether it is swallowed or spat out."[114]

Physicians will always be involved in abortion, if there is to be abortion, particularly in the cases of rape and incest. Since he is the person responsible for the act of abortion and since abortion promoters are always trying to reduce the number of people involved in an abortion,[115] more and more emphasis will be placed on his judgment in handling incestuous pregnancies. With recent legislation mandating professionals, including physicians, to report child abuse cases to public authorities, there is also an expectation that "his opinions will count heavily with the local agency in determining how the case will be handled."[116] If the physician happens to do abortions will he not render an opinion for an abortion if confronted with an incestuous pregnancy? Could this involve a conflict of interest, since public funding for abortion may be obtained by him for performing the abortion? What if all incest cases in a county have to be referred to one program whose medical director favors routine abortion for such cases? Is there any good reason to think that a viable alternative may be offered to the girl in light of the official abdication of the Hippocratic oath by organized medicine?[117]

The Dead End of Incestuous Abortion

If the incestuous family is turned into itself so as to keep its members from contributing to society at large, the incestuous pregnancy offers a ray of generosity to the world, a new life. To snuff it out by abortion is to compound the sexual child abuse with physical child abuse. A correlation between the number of abortions and the number of child abuse cases has been observed in England and the United States; namely, that child abuse has increased tenfold over the number of abortions in the last decade. John Linklater wrote in the *Spectator* that "the increase in the incidence of battering babies closely parallels the rising abortion rate, which suggests rather that the (English) Abortion Act (of 1967) encourages a ruthless attitude toward the troublesome infant."[118] The same correlation is seen in Colorado, the first state to liberalize abortion and one that clearly authorized abortion for incest. In this state the abortions and child abuse cases both rose about tenfold within a five-year period after the liberalization of abortion.[119] If a parent has the right to kill a child within the womb, should the child prove inconvenient, what further abuse can be heaped upon the child whose visible presence proves even more inconvenient? We have seen how incestuous fathers further assault their daughters by aborting the evidence of the incest. We have also seen how girls pregnant by incest resist this further assault upon their sexual integrity and take a step toward accepting responsibility for their sexual acts and thereby toward the freedom from the self-destructive effects of both incest and abortion.

While churchmen in England based their stand on incestuous abortion on the girl's "irremovable inability to acknowledge the child with which she was pregnant to be hers and that she would be overcome by the threat of it,"[120] the girls themselves are presented with undeniable evidence of their sexual activity, which they must acknowledge or else be overcome by the threat of their own sexual inclinations. They may try to eat away their sexual feelings and become obese; disperse these feelings among many men or women and become promiscuous or homosexual; convert them into a business venture and become prostitutes; or attempt to silence them by drugs, alcohol, or suicide attempts. They may even try to deny them by eliminating the fruit of their sexual activity and abort, but they will not be fulfilling themselves thereby. Contrary to the Church Assembly Board of Social Responsibility of the Church of England, which doomed them to a "determined rejection and resentment of the child, an invincible aversion," and denying their freedom and growth in love, these women need the reassuring and idealistic expectation of those who work with them.[121] Giarretto includes these girls as fullfledged members of society when he states that "caring is a practical and biologically determined need." "If mankind did not care for its children," he said, "the human species would die." He issues a dire warning that any society that does not provide for the needs of all its people must be classified as dysfunctional and will be eventually overwhelmed by its casualties.[122]

Certainly an incestuous pregnancy need not be left to the mother alone or to the incestuous parents or family to raise if they are not ready and willing to nurture it. As has been argued, a pregnant girl may look for nurturing in her child, rather than feel capable of providing nurturing for the child. Likewise, her parents taking over the care of her child may increase her feelings of deprivation and of being abused by them as their babymaking machine. But the least the incestuous family can do is protect the life of the child, accepting this responsibility while the child is dependent for its very life on the daughter. Until recently, our courts had recognized that "a child is in existence from the moment of conception,"[123] and that, moreover, "the right to life is inalienable in our society [and that there is no] necessity of balancing the mother's life against that of her child [because] the sanctity of the single human life is the decisive factor."[124] However, the U.S. Supreme

Court has overruled this fundamental opinion of the New Jersey State Court and a former defender of this doctrine, Rep. Robert Drinan,[125] a Jesuit priest, has become a dedicated foe to reinstituting this value of human life in our society.

As socially inappropriate as incest and incestuous pregnancies are, their harmful effects depend largely on reaction of others to the discovery of the incest as reported by incest workers over the past 70 years.[127] If society and its agents will accept and deal openly with consequences of the behavior of its citizens, the incestuous partners may likewise be encouraged to accept the responsibility for their behavior and modify it according to the natural function of the family. If social agents reject the consequences of the incestuous pregnancy by abortion, they are promoting the denial with its sequelae of the incest, including abortion, and are betraying the trust of every person in our society that all people will be protected.

Even if the incestuous offspring are not adopted by a stable family and "show no signs of becoming productive citizens . . . they are here—we cannot undo their existence."[128] These are sentiments of Dr. Vincent J. Fontana, chairman of the New York Mayor's Task Force on Child Abuse and Neglect, who sees abortion as a superficial answer to incest. He comments:

> In search of a quick and easy solution to the ugly reality of child abuse, a great many people have come up with glib answers based on the pill and other birth-control devices, planned parenthood, vasectomies, and abortions for the asking. Abortion is the favorite theme of the moment. The thrust of the argument is, of course, toward the prevention of child battering, neglect, and abuse through the prevention of children.[129]

> There are no short cuts, such as abortion, that lead to the answer of the problem of child abuse.[130]

> Whether we are selfish or unselfish it has got to make more sense, if there is any humanity in us, to find ways to improve the quality of human life and enrich it for all of us with every means at our disposal rather than abort it so that we will have fewer human beings to worry about and answer for.[131]

Incestuous pregnancies will probably never amount to a large number, and abortions of them will be even fewer. Yet they provide the touchstone to test the quality of our social life. If the only way we can help the little Debbies is to kill their babies and take away their fathers, are we not taking away the people for whom she cares the most? If her mother rallies to her side only to get rid of her father and child, isn't the pattern of avoiding problems being perpetuated? Can such a destructive mother-daughter alliance be satisfying to anyone? Doing away with people becomes another form of doing away with one's responsibility for what one is doing. Finally, left alone with the choice of either accepting responsibility for what one has done or doing away with oneself, we may expect a suicide to follow abortion as the quick and easy way to solving personal problems.

What is involved in the abortion when an innocent unborn child is aborted? What of the incestuous father who has been taken away, leaving behind only the unborn child to suffer a worse fate than his, since he is only jailed but the child is killed? Are we reenacting the maternal rejection felt by the daughter which predisposed the incest situation, so that the daughter is dramatically demonstrating what she feels the mother has done to her? Are we indirectly killing the daughter who feels her child is an extension of herself?

Whatever else we may be doing by an abortion of an incestuous pregnancy, we are promoting mental illness by not allowing the girl to accept the consequences of her own acts. The illness is shared by all who would deny the life of the child conceived by the incestuous act. Accepting the pregnancy can be the first step to accepting the incest and making the changes to alter the family pattern so that it can be more productive rather than withholding and destructive.

Footnotes

1. Communicable Disease Center reports 14 and 15; see references in Maloof, G. "The Psychology of Sexual Decision-Making" Pt. 1, ref. 57.
2. Jermann, ref. 50; also Sackler, ref. 81.
3. Butman, ref. 9.
4. Vincent, ref. 92; also Rosenthal, ref. 79.
5. Fink, ref. 27.
6. Young, ref. 95.
7. *S. F. Exam*, refs. 61 and 87.
8. Hamilton, ref. 42.
9. Visotsky, ref. 93.
10. Everstine, ref. 26.

11. Myers, ref. 63.
12. Diamond, ref. 24; also Sims, ref. 85.
13. Giarretto, ref. 34.
14. Colman, ref. 18.
15. DeFrancis, ref. 21.
16. Maisch, ref. 55.
17. Tormes, ref. 90.
18. Maisch, ref. 55.
19. Pollack, ref. 70.
20. Greenberg, ref. 38; also Pollack, ref. 70, p. 122.
21. Maloof, ref. 56; also Pollack, *ibid.*
22. Tormes, ref. 90, pp. 11-12.
23. Fontana, ref. 29.
24. Gentry, ref. 32.
25. Butler, ref. 8, p. 112.
26. Herman, ref. 44.
27. Giarretto, ref. 34.
28. Maisch, ref. 55.
29. Butler, ref. 8.
30. Glasser, ref. 36.
31. Risch, ref. 75.
32. Butler, ref. 8.
33. Cansino, ref. 15.
34. Butler, ref. 8, p. 47.
35. Colman, ref. 18.
36. Giarretto, ref. 34.
37. Glasser, ref. 36.
38. Myers, ref. 63.
39. Maisch, ref. 55.
40. Butler, ref. 8, pp. 41-2.
41. Risch, ref. 75.
42. Silverman, ref. 83.
43. Fontana, ref. 29, p. 49.
44. Adams, ref. 2.
45. Myers, ref. 63.
46. Maisch, ref. 55, p. 210.
47. Giarretto, ref. 34; also Colman, ref. 18.
48. Myers, ref. 63.
49. Jacobovitz, ref. 48, p. 143.
50. Veevers, ref. 91; also NON, ref. 64.
51. Devereux, ref. 23.
52. Delaney, ref. 22.
53. Noonan, ref. 66; also Callahan, ref. 14.
54. California Report, ref. 13.
55. Maisch, ref. 55, p. 40.

56. Devereux, ref. 23.
57. Devereux, ref. 23, p. 142.
58. Devereux, ref. 23.
59. Maisch, ref. 55; also Myers, ref. 63; Giarretto, ref. 34; Gentry, ref. 32.
60. Maisch, ref. 55.
61. Giarretto, ref. 34.
62. Goldsmith, ref. 37.
63. *S. F. Exam*, ref. 6 and 41.
64. Goldsmith, ref. 37.
65. Overstreet, ref. 67, p. 131.
66. Russell, ref. 80.
67. Hall, ref. 39.
68. Roemer, ref. 76, p. 289.
69. Medi-Cal, ref. 12.
70. Colman, ref. 18.
71. Medical Protection, ref. 60.
72. George, ref. 33, p. 28.
73. Sarvis, ref. 82, p. 80.
74. Anderson, ref. 4.
75. Sloane, ref. 86.
76. Calderone, ref. 10, p. 175.
77. Rosen, ref. 77.
78. Rosen, *ibid*; also Heffernan, ref. 43.
79. Ingram, ref. 47.
80. Hall, ref. 39, p. 63.
81. Rosenberg, ref. 78; also Geijerstam, ref. 31.
82. Hook, ref. 45; Aren, ref. 5; Calderone, ref. 10, p. 140.
83. Simon, ref. 84, p. 86.
84. Devereux, ref. 23, p. 52.
85. GAP, ref. 46; NCPS, ref. 11.
86. Williams, ref. 94, pp. 164-5.
87. *AMAN*, ref. 59.
88. *S. F. Exam*, ref. 3.
89. Tichero, ref. 89.
90. Lucas, ref. 54.
91. Murphy, ref. 62.
92. Donohue, ref. 25.
93. Pazzotti, ref. 69.
94. Jenks, ref. 49.
95. Lewit, ref. 52.
96. Sarvis, ref. 82, p. 81.
97. Phelan, ref. 68.
98. Maisch, ref. 55; also Tormes, ref. 90.

99. Friedman, C., ref. 30.
100. Kaltreider, ref. 51.
101. Myers, ref. 63.
102. Colman, ref. 18.
103. Rosenthal, ref. 79.
104. Fishman, ref. 28.
105. Burgess, ref. 7, p. 172.
106. Martin, C., ref. 58.
107. Denes, ref. 20.
108. Calderone, ref. 10.
109. Calderone, ref. 10, p. 121.
110. Hall, ref. 39, p. 109.
111. Randall, ref. 73.
112. Remsberg, ref. 74.
113. Kaltreider, ref. 51.
114. Denes, ref. 20 p. 5.
115. Hall, ref. 40.
116. MediCal, ref. 88.
117. *AMAN*, ref. 1.
118. Linklater, ref. 53.
119. *Crusade*, ref. 19; *Seattle Times*, ref. 17; *Washington Post*, ref. 16.
120. Ramsey, ref. 72.
121. Ramsey, *ibid*.
122. Giarretto, ref. 35.
123. Quay, ref. 71, p. 149.
124. Quay, *ibid*.
125. Hall, ref. 40, p. 230.
126. *NRLN*, ref. 65.
127. Maisch, ref. 55, p. 208.
128. Fontana, ref. 29, p. 242.
129. Fontana, ref. 29, p. 239.
130. Fontana, ref. 29, p. 241.
131. Fontana, ref. 29, p. 243.

References

1. "The Abortion Decision." Editorial *American Medical Association News*. September 19, 1977.
2. Adams, M. S., and Neal, J. V. "Children of Incest." *Pediatrics* 40 (1967): 55.

3. "Almost No Abortion Aid Survives Rush to Quit." *San Francisco Examiner*. October 18, 1978.

4. Anderson, E. W. "Psychiatric Indications for the Termination of Pregnancy." *World Medical Journal* 13: 81-83, May-June, 1966.

5. Aren, P., and Amark, C. "The Prognosis in Cases in which Legal Abortion Has Been Granted but Not Carried Out." *Acta Psychiatrica Scandinavica* 36 (1961): 203.

6. "Brown Signs Bills on State Bar, Contraceptives, Bingo, Schools." *San Francisco Examiner*. September 20, 1975.

7. Burgess, Ann, and Holstrom, L. "Interviewing Young Victims." In Burgess, et al., *Sexual Assault*.

8. Butler, Sandra. *Conspiracy of Silence: The Trauma of Incest.* San Francisco: New Glide Publications, 1978.

9. Butman, J. W. "Summary, Conclusions, and Implications." In *The Social, Psychological, and Behavioral World of the Teenage Girl*. Final Report to the Department of Health Education, and Welfare, Social Security Admin., June, 1965.

10. Calderone, Mary, ed. *Abortion in the United States*. New York: Harper, 1958.

11. "California Psychiatric Society Supports Abortion Funding." *Northern California Psychiatric Society Newsletter*. November 1977.

12. California State Department of Health Services. "Changes in Medi-Cal Funded Abortions." Letter of Beverlee A. Myers, Director. July 11, 1978.

13. California State Department of Public Health, Bureau of Maternal and Child Health. *Report to the Legislature on the Implementation of the 1967 Therapeutic Abortion Act*. Berkeley, 1971.

14. Callahan, Daniel. *Abortion: Law, Choice and Morality*. London: MacMillan Co., 1967.

15. Cansino, Karen, Coordinator of San Mateo County's Incest Treatment Program. Telephone Communication. September 7, 1978.

16. "Child Abuse Epidemic, HEW Says." *Washington Post*. December 2, 1975.

17. "Child Abuse Up 50-60% in Kings County." *Seattle Times*. September 22, 1974.

18. Colman, Peter. Telephone Communication. September 11, 1978.

19. *Crusade for Life.* Vol. 11, No. 3, October 1976.

20. Denes, Magda. "Performing Abortions." *Reflections* Vol. XII, No. 5, 1977.

21. De Francis, V. *Protecting the Child Victim of Sex Crimes Committed by Adults: Final Report.* Denver: American Humane Association, 1969.

22. Delaney, James J. "New Concepts of the Family Court." Chapter 17 in Helfer, Ray E. and Kempe, C. Henry, eds. *Child Abuse and Neglect.* Cambridge, Mass.: Ballinger Pub. Co., 1976.

23. Devereux, George. *A Study of Abortion in Primitive Societies.* Revised Edition. New York: International Universities Press, Inc., 1976.

24. Diamond, S. E. "ISMS Symposium on Medical Implications of the Current Abortion Law in Illinois." *Illinois Medical Journal.* May, 1967, pp. 677-80.

25. Donohue, Michael. Major, Pennsylvania State Police. "Letter to Rep. Daniel J. Flood, July 14, 1977." In National Committee for a Human Life Amendment, Inc. *Arguments in Support of Oberster/Hyde Amendment (Section 209) to the 1979 Labor-HEW Appropriations Bill.* Washington, D.C., 1978.

26. Everstine, Diana S. "Incest." Paper presented at the Third Don D. Jackson Memorial Conference on "Human Problems: Ordinary and Extraordinary." San Francisco, June 30-July 1, 1978.

27. Fink, Judith. "Advisor Urges 'Total Approach' to Quell Teenage Pregnancy Rate." *ACCL Update.* April, 1977.

28. Fishman, Susan H. "Factors Associated with the Decision of Unwed Pregnant Adolescents to Deliver or Abort." Paper delivered at the annual meeting of the American Public Health Association, October 1976.

29. Fontana, Vincent A. *Somewhere a Child Is Crying: Maltreatment—Causes and Prevention.* New York: MacMillan & Co., 1973.

30. Friedman, Cornelia; Greenspan, Rhoda; and Mittelman, Faye. "The Decision-Making Process and the Outcome of Therapeutic Abortion." Paper presented at the 1974 annual meeting of the American Psychiatric Association, Detroit, June 1974.

31. Geijerstam, A. F. in Calderone, Mary, ed. *Abortion in the United States.* New York: Harper, 1958.

32. Gentry, Charles E. Executive Director of Child and Family Services, Knoxville, Tenn. Correspondence, August 25, 1978.

33. George, B. James, Jr. "Current Abortion Laws: Proposals and Movements for Reform." In *Abortion and the Law*, Smith, David, T. ed. Cleveland: Western Reserve U. Press, 1967.

34. Giarretto, Henry. Telephone Communication, August 14, 1978.

35. Giarretto, Henry, et al. Chapter 14 in Burgess, et al. *Sexual Assault.*

36. Glasser, Martin, M. D. Medical Director, San Francisco Child Sex Abuse Treatment Program. Personal Communication, July 21, 1978.

37. Goldsmith, Sadja; Gabrielson, Mary O.; Gabrielson, Ira; Matthews, Vicki; and Potts, Leah. "Teenagers, Sex, and Contraception." *Family Planning Perspectives.* 4, No. 1, (January 1972): 32-38.

38. Greenberg, N. H.; Loesch, J.; and Lakin, M. "Life Situations Associated with Onset of Pregnancy." *Psychosomatic Medicine.* 21 (1959): 246.

39. Hall, Robert E., ed. *Abortion in a Changing World.* Vol. II. New York and London: Columbia U. Press, 1970.

40. Hall, Robert. "Commentary." In *Abortion and the Law*, Smith, David T., ed.

41. Hamilton, Mildred. "Minor's Right in Abortion." *San Francisco Examiner.* October 4, 1973, quoting Judith Kleinberg, a San Francisco lawyer.

42. Hamilton, Mildred. "Teenage Pregnancy: Elaine Grady of the San Francisco Schools Special Service Center." *San Francisco Examiner.* February 15, 1973, p. 24.

43. Hefferman, Roy J. and Lynch, William A. "What is the Status of Therapeutic Abortion in Modern Obstetrics?" *American Journal of Obstetrics and Gynecology.* August 1953, p. 335, ff.

44. Herman, Judith, and Hirschman, Lisa. "Father-Daughter Incest." *Signs: Journal of Women in Culture and Society.* 2, No. 4 (1977): 735-56.

45. Hook, Kersten. "Refused Abortion: A Follow-up Study of 249 Women Whose Applications Were Refused by the National Board of Health in Sweden." *Acta Psychiatrica Scandinavica.* Vol. 39, Supp., 168, 1963.

46. *Humane Reproduction.* Vol. VIII, Report No. 86. New York: Group for the Advancement of Psychiatry. August 1973.

47. Ingram, James, et al. "Interruption of Pregnancy for Psychiatric Indication: A Suggested Method of Control." *Obstetrics and Gynecology.* Vol. 29, No. 2, February 1967, p. 251.

48. Jacobvitz, Immanuel. "Jewish Views on Abortion." Chapter 6 in *Abortion and the Law*. Smith, David T.

49. Jenks, Paul C. "530 Second-Trimester Abortions Done Safely." *Medical World News.* May 20, 1974.

50. Jermann, Thomas C. "It's Time to Defuse Population Explosionists." *The National Observer.* July 27, 1978, p. 10.

51. Kaltreider, Nancy, "Impact of Late Abortion on Patients and Staff." Paper presented at the annual spring meeting of the Northern California Psychiatric Association, Yosemite Park, Calif., April 1978.

52. Lewit, Sarah. "Early Medical Complications of Legal Abortion." In *Abortion in the Clinic and Office Setting*, Hart, Thomas.

53. Linklater, John. Medical Column. *Spectator.* August 10, 1974.

54. Lucas, Ferris B. Executive Director of the National Sheriff's Association. "Letter to Honorable Henry J. Hyde, M.C., July 18, 1977." In *Arguments in Support of Oberster/Hyde Amendment.*

55. Maisch, Herbert. *Incest.* Translated by Colin Beame. New York: Stein and Day Publications, 1972.

56. Maloof, George. "The Value of Human Life." *Marriage and Family Newsletter.* Vol. 6, Nos. 10-12, 1975.

57. Maloof, George. "The Psychology of Sexual Decision Making." *International Review of Natural Family Planning.* Vol. 1, No. 3, 1977.

58. Martin, Cynthia. "Seeker of Alternatives to Abortion: Abortion Is a Lousy Method of Birth Control." *San Francisco Examiner.* November 12, 1973.

59. "Massachusetts Abortion Rules Are Blocked by Federal Judge." *American Medical Association News.* August 18, 1978.

60. Medical Protection Society, The. *The Abortion Act 1967.* London: Pittman Medical Publishing Co., 1969.

61. "More Teen Girls Have Sex." *San Francisco Examiner.* April 17, 1977.

62. Murphy, Glen R., Director, Bureau of Governmental Relations and Legal Counsel, International Association of Chiefs of Police, Inc. "Letter to Hon. Henry J. Hyde, M. C., July 18, 1977." In *Arguments in Support of Oberster/Hyde Amendment.*

63. Myers, Barbara. Telephone Communication, August 18, 1978.

64. National Organization of Non-Parents, Peter Scales, Teen Pro-

ject and Public Affairs Director. "Statement of Principles." Press Release. January 1978.

65. *National Right to Life News.* July 1978.

66. Noonan, John T., ed. *The Morality of Abortion: Legal and Historical Perspectives.* Cambridge, Mass.: Harvard U. Press, 1970.

67. Overstreet, Edmund W. "Experience with the New California Law." In *Abortion in a Changing World.* Hall, ed.

68. Phelan, Lana and Maginnis, Patricia. *The Abortion Handbook for Responsible Women.* Canoga Park, Calif.: Weiss, Day and Lord, 1969.

69. *Playboy.* December 1975.

70. Pollack, Otto, and Friedman, Alfred S., eds. *Family Dynamics and Female Sexual Delinquency.* Palo Alto, Calif.: Science and Behavior Books, 1969, p. 62.

71. Quay, P. "Justifiable Abortion: Medical and Legal Foundations." *Georgetown Law Journal* 49: 173, pp. 233-25, 1960.

72. Ramsey, Paul. "Reference Points in Deciding About Abortion." In *The Morality of Abortion*, Noonan.

73. Randall, Clyde. Prof. of OB-GYN at State Univ. of New York Medical School at Buffalo. "Abortion and Obstetrics." In *Abortion in a Changing World,* Hall.

74. Remsberg, Charles, and Remsberg, Bonnie. "Second Thoughts About Abortion." *Good Housekeeping.* March 1976. In *Conservative Digest.* September 1976, pp. 32-33.

75. Robey, Ames. "The Runaway Girl." In *Family Dynamics*, Pollack and Friedman, Chapter 12.

76. Roemer, Ruth. "Legalization of Abortion in the U.S." In *The Abortion Experience: Psychological and Medical Impact.* Osofsky, Howard J., and Osofsky, Joy D. Hagerstown, Md.: Harper and Row, 1973.

77. Rosen, Harold. *Therapeutic Abortion.* Philadelphia: Julian Press, 1954.

78. Rosenberg, Allen, and Silver, Emmanuel. "Suicide, Psychiatrists, and Therapeutic Abortion." *California Medicine* 102: 1965, p. 407.

79. Rosenthal, Miriam, and Rothchild, Ellen. "Psychological Considerations in Adolescent Pregnancy and Abortion." Paper delivered at the annual meeting of the American Association of Planned Parenthood Physicians. April 1974, Memphis.

80. Russell, Keith. "Therapeutic Abortion: The California Experience." In *The Abortion Experience*. Osofsky.

81. Sackler, Arthur M. "The ZPG Tide Is Changing." *Medical Tribune*. November 3, 1976.

82. Sarvis, Betty, and Rodman, Hyman. *The Abortion Controversy*. New York and London: Columbia U. Press, 1974.

83. Silverman, Arthur. Clinical Director, Youth Team, North San Mateo County Mental Health Center, Daly City, Calif. Personal Communication, May 9, 1978.

84. Simon, Nathan M. "Psychological and Emotional Indications for Therapeutic Abortion." In *Abortion: Changing Views and Practice*. Sloane.

85. Sims, B. M. "A District Attorney Looks at Abortion." A Buffalo, N. Y., 1969 study revealing no pregnancy from confirmed rape in 30 years. Reported in *Child and Family* 8: 176-180, Spring, 1969.

86. Sloane, R. Bruce, ed. *Abortion: Changing Views and Practice*. New York and London: Grune and Stratton, 1971.

87. "Society Accepting Unwed Motherhood." *San Francisco Examiner*. June 3, 1976.

88. "Suspected Child Abuse Cases." *Medical Bulletin*. July 1978.

89. Tichero, Midge. California State Department of Health, Center for Health Statistics, Berkeley, Calif. Telephone Communication, November 11, 1978.

90. Tormes, Yvonne M. *Child Victims of Incest*. Denver: The American Humane Association, Children's Division, 1968.

91. Veevers, J. E. "Voluntary Childlessness and Social Policy: An Alternative View." *The Family Coordinator*. October 1974, pp. 397-406.

92. Vincent, C. E. *Unmarried Mothers*. New York: Free Press, 1961.

93. Visotsky, Harold M. "A Community Project for Unwed Pregnant Adolescents." In *Family Dynamics*, Pollack and Friedman.

94. Williams, George Huntston. "The Sacred Condominium." In *The Morality of Abortion*. Noonan.

95. Young, L. R. "Personality Patterns in Unmarried Mothers." In *Understanding the Psychology of the Unmarried Mother*. New York: Family Service Agency of America, 1947.

Psychic Causes and Consequences of the Abortion Mentality

Conrad W. Baars, M.D.

There are three questions concerning induced abortions which deserve serious attention, though not necessarily all of them at this conference.

1. Is induced abortion, whether to save the life of the mother, or to safeguard her physical and psychic health, morally justified?

2. Is induced abortion psychologically justified, i.e., does it safeguard or even promote her "mental health" or could it have psychological ill effects on the mother and/or society?

3. Is its legality in this or any country justified, i.e., is making abortion readily accessible truly for the common good, or could it, especially when performed on a large scale, be detrimental to society?

I do not believe that we need to concern ourselves any longer with, "When does life begin?", since we have enough scientific evidence that human life is a continuum and that individual personhood begins at the moment of conception.

The psychological stresses commonly given as indications for induced abortion may be divided into two groups. Incest and rape pregnancies, pregnancies in women suffering from some form of mental illness, and pregnancies precipitating depression or other psychopathological states in "normal" women. These last states often overlap with less well-defined syndromes, resulting from a pregnancy, but create worry, tension and concern because of the socio-economic burden the pregnancy imposes; because the child is not wanted; because the mother is too young or immature; because there is no husband to support the mother; because of the possible presence of a birth defect; because of parental pressure to get rid of the pregnancy; because the mother is counseled to exercise her right to choose, to show her independence and emancipation, or to do her part in not contributing to the alleged threat of overpopulation, and so on.

Abortion and Mental Health

I shall confine myself to a discussion of the question, "What effect does the deliberate killing of an innocent human being have in principle—regardless of reasons of real or alleged psychological stress precipitated by the pregnancy—on the 'mental health' of the mother?" I hope to present arguments and principles that will enable us also to answer the questions concerning the effects on the "mental health" of persons advocating abortion, performing abortions, and assisting in them and on the "mental health" of society that legalizes abortion for non-life-threatening reasons, utilitarian reasons and reasons of convenience.

Indispensable to the task of answering my afore-mentioned question is, of course, a sound definition of "mental health." The problem is that no such definition of "mental health" exists. It seems likely that this is one of the reasons why there are no uniform scientific data about the psychological effects of induced abortions on the mother who requests, demands, or is persuaded to undergo an abortion. I am not aware of any great and urgent desire on the part of abortion advocates, not even among those who are members of the American Psychiatric Association or American Psychological Association, to gather scientific support for their claims that the "mental health" of the majority of women is not adversely affected by induced abortions.

Yet, a correct concept of "mental health" is important, not only for the sake of gauging the actual psychological effects of abortion on the mother of the child killed before birth, but also because it may well be that the "mental health" of a society, or the relative or absolute lack of it, has a direct bearing on the fact that our society, indeed, our world, considers it necessary to do now what it has abhorred through the centuries. Although this is not the time or the place to explain this, there is no doubt in my mind that our society's "mental ill-health" has a direct bearing on our present abortion mentality, and represents a cause-and-effect link with such seemingly unrelated developments as water and air pollution, waste of food and energy resources, monetary debasement and inflation, greater immorality, violence and sexual promiscuity, as well as the other ills of the Western world spotlighted by Alexander Solzhenitsyn in his June 1978 Harvard address.[1]

Mental Health and Psychic Wholeness

What, then, is "mental health"?

No one will dispute that "mental health" is something more than the absence of mental illness, just as peace is much more than the absence of war.

If we know so much about mental illness, how is it possible that we know so little about "mental health"? Could it be that human scientists by and large refuse to look at man in his entirety —a body-soul unit, a psychosomatic unit of which the psychic part consists of nonmaterial elements that cannot be measured scientifically? A semantic trick seems to support this contention. When physicians and human scientists consider themselves concerned solely with man's "mental health" and "physical health," they imply that man is composed of a body and a mind. The Latin word for "mind" is "mens," of which "mental" is a derivative. "Mens" or "mind" originally stood for his thinking faculty. But, since the emotional and the spiritual also contain thinking elements, the concept "mind" became expanded, though more vague. A more fitting word to describe the sum total of the emotional, mental, and spiritual levels of man is the Greek word "psyche." It means "soul." Whoever coined the words "psychiatry" and "psychology" knew intuitively—a manner of knowing to which I shall come back shortly—that the study of man cannot be restricted to the purely material, scientifically measurable. If this is done anyway, then the words "mind" and "brain" are adequate, and do not remind us so readily of the fact that we exclude a certain dimension of man.

Psychology—The Study of Man as Man

In attempting to arrive at an acceptable definition of "psychic wholeness," I shall describe the components of man's psyche— namely, the spiritual faculty, the intellectual and volitional faculties, and the faculty that constitutes the link between these higher faculties and the body—man's emotional life, which has in each and every one of its emotions a psychological as well as a physiological aspect. If, in doing so, it is necessary to refer to a Creator of man, I shall do so without apology. If in the minds of some this will be considered "unscientific," then so be it.

With the rejection by American psychology of the language, concepts, and philosophic foundations of European psychology, and the virtual absence of faculty psychology for the past one-half century, no progress has been made in this country in defining the concept of "mental health." This, of course, is not surprising in a psychology which views human behavior as a complex integration of basic biological needs and essential cultural adaptation. The functions of man's brain, mind and emotions, poorly understood and defined as they are, contribute little to a workable definition of "mental health." Of these three factors, we know most about the workings of the brain. However, with no acknowledgment of a qualitative difference between human and animal intelligence, the psychologists define human intelligence as that which is measured by their intelligence tests! Much less is said about man's free will, if it is taken into consideration at all. And, despite the wide attention given man's emotions, their function is not clearly defined, whether in themselves or in their relationship to the intellect and will.

What is the solution to this apparent dilemma? In my opinion, a marriage between American and European psychology, however belated, can provide us with an expanded view of human cognition and conation which enables us to define "psychic wholeness" and "psychic illness" in an intellectually satisfying and clinically practical way. Moreover, this approach makes it possible to recognize an in-between state of "psychic debility," not recognizable or definable in current "mental health" terminology. It is this state of "psychic debility" which, while masquerading as "mental health," underlies our abortion and euthanasia mentality, as well as the other major national and global problems alluded to before.

Emotions—Man's Psychic Motors

Human emotions are psychic motors producing two different kinds of motion or movement. The inner motion caused by the first group of emotions is comparable to that produced in a light bulb when we flip the switch. The movement of electrons creates light and warmth. And so it is with this group of the "humane emotions" which are aroused by our external senses and the internal sense of the imagination. Emotions like love, joy, sadness, compassion, and tenderness belong to this group.

Since all emotions by their very nature function primarily for the good of their owner, they become other-oriented under the ennobling influence of a higher human faculty, man's intellect. While his senses provide him only with particular, concrete knowledge of the world around him, his intellect gives him universal or abstract knowledge about the essence of particular or concrete things, about truth and the meaning of his existence and his relationship to other human beings and God. A child finds joy in the toys he loves and because they are his, and not someone's else's. As a mature father, he will feel even greater joy in his wife and children being happy with the things he has provided for them. He is capable of experiencing compassion, tenderness, kindness, affection, unselfish love, and concern for others.

The second group of emotions stimulate man to move outward, to act, to do things, to speak, to labor, to walk or run, and so on. These actions are directed at overcoming obstacles, at doing things that are hard and difficult and require effort. Or they are directed at protecting oneself or others against harmful things, against threats to one's life, or health, or peace of mind, or liberty. In short, their function and purpose is utilitarian in nature. The emotions of hope, despair, courage, and fear are four basic utilitarian emotions. Hope and courage are the optimistic, energetic ones; fear and despair are the pessimistic or anergic ones. Then there is a fourth emotion in this group, the ultimate emotion, so to speak, which stimulates man by means of an extra secretion of adrenaline to try and throw off the harm that has overcome him already. This is the emotion of anger. Their immediate source of stimulation is man's instincts, to a large extent conditioned early in life by his parents and others, and his memories of earlier useful or harmful situations.

The link between psyche and soma is provided by the physiological changes that take place simultaneously with the psychic awareness of an emotion. Although we are most familiar with the changes accompanying the emotions of fear and anger, they are no less an intrinsic part of the emotions of love, sadness, hope, joy, compassion, hate, etc. It is because of the fact that every human emotion has an inseparable psychic and physiological component that man always reacts as a psychosomatic unit.

Reason and Intellect

When we speak of the human mind, we think of man's rational faculty, his reason, which forms ideas, thoughts, judgments, comparisons, analyses, and so on. This is man's thinking or discursive mind. We are much less familiar with a second source of knowledge. This cognitive source has a receiving character. It receives its knowledge as a gift, most often when we are in a state of quiet, relaxed, just prior to falling asleep; or when we are "engaged" in worldly or spiritual contemplation. This receiving source of knowledge is the intellect in its narrower meaning of "inter-legere," i.e., "reading between" the lines. It is man's intuitive, contemplative, or gifted mind. Its chief sources of knowledge are nature, the arts, faith, and God. All of them can give us knowledge beyond and superior to what is actually seen, heard, read, or meditated upon. If man possesses an actual spiritual faculty, it would be his intuitive mind.

Free Will

The other psychic faculty is that of free will. Its function is to choose, on the basis of the information presented by reason, what course of action man will take. Not yet free in the child, it gradually becomes free during the process of growing to maturity, provided, of course, that he is not afflicted with emotional illness, mental disorder, organic brain disease, or mental retardation, to mention the most important causes of possible interference with the freedom of man's will.

"Heart" and "Mind"

How are the two groups of emotions and the higher faculties related to one another, qua function and qua order of importance? The humane emotions are closely related to, and work intimately together with, the intuitive mind; the utilitarian emotions with our thinking mind. Intuition and humane emotions have to do primarily with the good, the beautiful, and the truth; with love and joy in friendship and marriage; with sadness, suffering, and compassionate caring; with matters of faith and God; with all that contributes, or fails to contribute, to man's authentic happiness in relationship with himself, others, and God.

Our thinking mind and utilitarian emotions have to do with solving problems; with being efficient and practical; with achievement, building, technology; with training skills; with all that is useful or harmful. They are, when successful, the source of much satisfaction and rightful pride; of comforts and pleasures and a happiness which is of a lower order than "authentic happiness."

In the order of importance our intuition and humane emotions —man's "heart"—rank first, our thinking mind and utilitarian emotions—man's "mind"—second. The "mind" must serve the "heart," man's primary faculty of joy and happiness, not the other way around. We are created for happiness, to share in the infinite happiness of our Creator. The greater our knowledge of what is good for our human nature, the stronger and more successful our will in striving for it, the greater our happiness. But this happiness cannot be experienced fully without the emotions of love and joy and the other humane emotions.

Our emotions have an innate need to be respected and guided by reason. Whenever they are frustrated in this need, there results a psychological disturbance. When the useful is done for its own sake, and not for the purpose of obtaining something we love and desire, we will not experience the joy of possessing that thing.

Our capacity for being moved, as only a human being can be

moved, our "affectivity," takes precedence over our "effectivity," our capacity for doing.

In all this it is not a matter of either/or, of either intuition or reason, of either humane or utilitarian emotions, of either affectivity or effectivity, but of both, though always in their proper order and interdependence.

When a person's will, informed by reason, opts for the good, and it is supported by the emotion of desire for that good, a person possesses true "will power." However, when the will has been trained, for whatever reasons, to battle the emotions, he must "force the will," a process in which much energy is expended that could be used for better purposes. This has always been considered virtue in those philosophies or religions which hold that man's nature is corrupt and tends toward evil.

Only philosophies or religions which hold that man is oriented toward the good, even since the Fall, though in an imperfect manner, make it possible for him to develop true will power, live a virtuous life of a higher order and make him less vulnerable to psychic trauma. Unlike the former philosophies and religious beliefs, the latter do not constitute of themselves an obstacle to man's need to develop psychic wholeness.

Psychic Wholeness and Psychic Debility

A person may be said to enjoy psychic wholeness when he possesses a fully developed and harmoniously balanced "heart" and "mind," while the will is free to choose the good insofar as it is known.

Persons possessing this psychic wholeness are psychically strong and are a source of strength for others. In fact, it is this psychic strength alone which enables a child to become the adult he is supposed to be, to possess himself, to be his own person.

If he does not receive this psychic strength, he will feel unloved, insignificant, worthless, inferior, inadequate, and insecure. These symptoms are those of what we have called the "unaffirmed person."[2] He is psychically weak, emotionally like a child, and incapable of being authentically present to others and to reveal to them their unique goodness and worthwhileness. This manner of being present to others and all that is, with the full attention of one's whole being, I call "affirming living." It is *the* source of joy, peace, happiness, and strength for the person himself, as well as for all so fortunate to live in the orbit of his affirming love.

This concept of psychic wholeness is at the root of a new

understanding of the different kinds of neuroses and provides appropriate and successful therapies. Of equal importance is the fact that it lets us differentiate between emotional maturity and immaturity, between psychic wholeness and the subclinical entity of psychic debility. I will explain this in reference to our present abortion mentality.

Pursuit of Happiness

Reaching back to the beginnings of our country, you will recall that the Declaration of Independence guaranteed its citizens the right to life, liberty, and the pursuit of happiness. I am inclined to believe that the particular phrasing of this third right set in motion the process by which millions are denied each year the first right, and all of us are in danger of losing the second. Happiness, true happiness, it should be realized, cannot be pursued. It is a gift we receive when another person loves us in an unselfish manner, when we have true friends, when we live according to the laws of our nature and of God. The happiness we experience as the result of our successful activities, material gains, technological advances, and so on, is of a lesser order. I shall refer to it with the term "pseudo-happiness."

To the extent that pseudo-happiness is and remains subordinate to our true happiness, all is well. However, it is a different matter when our striving and doing assume proportions that stifle our state of affectivity, which determines and enriches our living in right relationships with self, others, and God. Or, to say it in other words, when our utilitarian emotions hypertrophy at the expense of a growing atrophy of our humane emotions.

Repressive Neuroses

I believe that this unbalanced psychic process has prevailed for many, many generations in our country and the Western world, aided and abetted by the Protestant work ethic and Christian people's long-standing fear and suspicion of man's lower nature, i.e., of his sense life and emotional life. The primary consequences of this ethic and fear are seen in the obsessive-compulsive neuroses, i.e., those neurotic conditions in which either fear or energy (our term for the utilitarian emotions of courage and hope) repress the humane emotions deemed dangerous.

With the growing incidence of this neurosis, which psychoanalytic therapy has not been capable of healing, the number of people without a healthy capacity to love, to be compassionate, to be affectionate, gentle and tender, to find joy and happiness in the joy of others, increased at an ever greater pace. Or, to say it differently, as the effectivity of our "mind" increasingly stifled the affectivity of our "heart"—our most precious, but also most fragile possession—we became more and more incapable of leading the affirming life. Because of the immutable fact that unaffirmed parents cannot help but raise unaffirmed children, generation after generation became weaker and weaker, its psychic debility greater and greater.

Deprivation Neurosis

As the number of repressive neurotics showed a steady decline the past several decades, psychiatrists began to see a growing number of "neurotic patients for whom appropriate diagnostic labels were lacking and in whom traditional exploratory psychotherapy proved ineffective as the unconscious seemed to have lost most of its mysterious and noxious quality."[3] It is this "puzzling neurotic caseload"[3] that is made up largely of persons who were not adequately affirmed by their parents. Most of them are to be found on the end of the spectrum of non-affirmation which we have labeled "deprivation neurosis."[2] Persons with this syndrome go to the psychiatrist with complaints of feeling unloved, lonely, inferior, inadequate, insecure, unable to make friends, fearful of the adult world in which they feel themselves like babies or children, and last but not least, depression. These prime candidates for suicide cannot be healed with conventional therapies—probing, drugs, E.T.T.—because they have never repressed unacceptable emotions. Healing will occur only when others can be present to them in an affirming manner. As this requires full emotional maturity on the part of already affirmed persons, the possibilities for healing threaten to diminish to the extent that our neurotic society would fail to be converted to greater psychic wholeness.

Self-Affirmation

On the other end of the spectrum we find the unaffirmed person who does not succumb to the feelings just described, but sets out to prove to himself and the world that he *is* significant, worthwhile, adequate, and equal. This self-affirming[4] person does this by using his "mind" to plot and manipulate others in trying to amass material goods, riches, power, fame, status symbols, and the like, which he expects will give him the feelings his parents failed to give him. In order to feel loved and wanted he uses others in sexual encounters. But as he is incapable of loving others unselfishly he fails in sex as miserably as he fails in feeling important, adequate, and significant by means of his utilitarian pursuits, even and precisely when they have brought him to the top of the ladder of success, or to the top of the mountain of power and fame. For him, too, suicide is often the only way out from a world where he was admired and befriended for what he *did*, never for what he *was*.

Of course, for the uninitiated it is indeed most difficult, if not impossible, to distinguish between the psychically weak self-affirming person and the reasonably mature, well-adjusted individual. As long as the public and the human scientists are unfamiliar with the syndromes of deprivation neurosis and self-affirmation, we will continue to believe that everyone who is not clinically a repressive neurotic or an obviously disabled deprivation neurotic, is "normal." Thus we will continue to believe that our society is much more normal than it really is.

Psychic Deprivation and Abortion Mentality

What is the connection between this subtle change from the psychic strength of the early settlers to the psychic weakness of recent generations and the sudden supplanting of centuries of respect for life and defense of the unborn by the merciless attack on defenseless children?

Deprivation neurotic mothers are and feel incapable of giving their children the love they never received themselves. In this real distress they become the all-too-ready victims of the abortion advocates, while the fathers of their children are usually also unaffirmed persons and lack the fortitude to stand up in defense of the unborn.

The more energetic and aggressive self-affirmed men and women are equally incapable of affirming their children. Unable or unwilling to face this weakness in themselves, they prevent it from becoming conscious by devising and promoting reasons why their children should not be born. Those self-affirming persons become the abortion advocates, the outspoken defenders of the "right to choose," the "heart"-less abortionists, the persons ready to betray their Hippocratic oath. Self-affirming pregnant women are the first to demand the right to abort the child they know or sense they are incapable of loving. The child must be sacrificed for the sake of preventing the shattering of a feeble self-image.

The present life-and-death struggle is a battle between the self-affirming abortion advocates and others devoid of what makes man truly human, the capacity to be moved with love and compassion, and the more or less adequately affirmed pro-lifers, with the emotionally crippled, totally unaffirmed, deprivation neurotic mothers as defenseless victims in the middle. Those desiring to familiarize themselves with the differences in personalities of the two types of unaffirmed persons will find it worth their while to study the profiles of the most outspoken abortion advocates as they appear in public gatherings, and compare them with the workers in emergency pregnancy centers, Birthright, pro-life, and related organizations.

Psychic Consequences of Induced Abortion

What effect does the actual abortion procedure have on the psyches of the persons involved? As their psyches are already weakened, it is hard to imagine that they could gain in strength from a procedure that denies instead of affirms the unborn his being. No amount of rationalization can hide successfully the telltale marks left on the psyche by the sacrificing of innocent human life for the purpose of utilitarian gains.

Denial, the very opposite of affirmation, can be rationalized away, but its effect on the self-affirming persons cannot be eradicated. Abortionists, whether performing their sinister work in hospitals or back alleys, get richer, but not happier or healthier. Their nursing assistants may receive the best training from psychiatrists and behavior modifiers to be desensitized to their natural feelings of compassion, but the emergence of feelings of guilt and depression cannot be suppressed forever. The self-affirming pregnant woman may be proud of having exercised her right to choose, but she cannot escape, any less than the non-pregnant abortion advocates can, the further weakening of her already wounded psyche. Society may pride itself on having devised a way of dealing with the alleged threat of overpopulation, but it cannot remain blind to the fact that it is committing suicide.

And what about the effect on the deprivation neurotic mother, who in her obvious psychic weakness, submits to the killing of her child?

The consequences of an induced abortion for such an unaffirmed woman, who is in fact emotionally immature and feels like a child, consist always of a deepening of her feelings of inferiority, inadequacy, insignificance, and worthlessness. These feelings may be supressed for a while as she is freed of the immediate stress of having to love her child and is exposed to a constant barrage of conditioning stimuli from a society that claims that she had a right to control her own body, that an abortion is a harmless procedure, that she must be proud of having done her part to combat the threat of overpopulation, and of not exposing an unwanted child to the trauma of not being loved. Yet, sooner or later, the truth will make itself known and felt, and the bitter realization that she was not even unselfish enough to share her life with another human being will take its toll. If she had ever entertained a doubt as to whether her parents and others really considered her unlovable and worthless, she will now be certain that she was indeed never any good in their eyes or her own. A deep depression will be inevitable and her preoccupation with thoughts of suicide that much greater.

All this holds true with even greater force for the countless unaffirmed pre-teen girls who are in desperate search for someone to love them. When they learn from personal experimentation that this cannot be found in sexual promiscuity, they often desire to have a child of their own, in the expectation that the child will give them what their parents failed to provide. No one can be blind to what must happen, and is happening these days all too often to unaffirmed youngsters, when other grown-ups prove to be just as pseudo-affirming or denying as their own parents, in their eagerness to persuade or force them to have an abortion. Such conduct constitutes psychic murder of these already deprived girls, and unless they are so fortunate to be helped by affirming persons, they will become the victims of a malignant depression. The effect on the psyche of unaffirmed boys and men responsible for their pregnancies is similar in nature, though clinically less evident when the syndrome of psychic debility is not known.

Authentic Help for the Pregnant Woman in Distress

If abortion is not the answer to a pregnancy that causes grave distress to the unaffirmed, deprivation neurotic woman, what is? Such a woman, whether married or single, is for all practical purposes always in need of help. Without such help it is most difficult, if not impossible, for her to cope with her situation. The only help worthy of the name is the unselfish love of others. Some persons appear sincere in their belief that the most loving thing is to provide an abortion for a woman who is truly incapable of caring for her child because she is so much like a child herself. But this is not true.

To affirm an unaffirmed, child-like pregnant woman, means to accept her in her helplessness and thus also to recognize that she is not guilty of her psychic inability to welcome the child in her womb. Such affirming help entails that it is made crystal clear to her that no one can and will demand that she welcome and affirm the child. In other words, the woman *may* be weak and needy. She does not have to be strong and self-sufficient. To let her *know* and *feel* this is affirmation of the highest order. For the unaffirmed woman to feel such compassionate understanding from a fellow human being is a gift of life.

Not infrequently such life-giving affirming presence is the very beginning of a newly developing psychic strength and of a desire to carry her child to term, the very child which at first she was unable to recognize as being a part of her own, imprisoned, unaffirmed being. Whether she should give her child up for adoption or raise it herself will depend, of course, on many factors — whether she is married or single, whether her husband is an affirming person, whether she will have an opportunity to live in the orbit of affirming persons, etc.

But to advise her, or to insist, that she have an abortion is tantamount to conveying to her that she is indeed the inferior, inadequate, and worthless person she had always felt she was, a person who could or would not even give the child within her its own life; could or would not even let her bodily processes carry on their natural functions, and put up with some bodily discomforts for a few months.

Abortion and Socio-Economic Stress

Finally, I want to briefly address the questions of whether serious socio-economic stresses, incest or rape, or a defective child are ever valid reasons for abortion.

Concerning the first question, that of grave socio-economic stress, a discussion is required only in cases of an affirmed pregnant woman, or a married couple, both of whom are affirmed. Authentic help for this woman consists again of affirmation, which means that she may be allowed to be who she is: a woman who is able and willing to affirm her unborn child. To advise or insist on an abortion would be to deny this woman her right and need to be a loving mother of her child, and therefore, this is not help worthy of the name.

Effective help for her consists of protecting her from the socio-economic burdens: poverty, debts, unemployment, inadequate living quarters, non-support by the father of the unborn child, society's demand that she have an abortion for society's sake, and so on. The realization that most of these socio-economic stresses and pressures are also the direct or indirect outcome of our society's growing psychic debility, is no excuse for abortion. It should impress on us even more profoundly how much people are in need of learning to live affirming lives.

The conclusion that socio-economic stress is never an indication for abortion in pregnant affirmed women, holds equally true for unaffirmed women. For them real help is first of all authentic affirmation, and, secondarily, protection from social and economic stresses. In either case one thus avoids the crippling psychic sequelae of abortion which sooner or later would make it even more difficult for these women to cope with those stresses.

Abortion and Rape

In the few instances when conception occurs when a man forces himself violently and with threat of death on a woman, the only good thing that results from this act of denial is the child. If this child were to be aborted, this good, too, would become the victim of denial. The rape together with the abortion become total denial to the point of nothingness.

The denial of the child cannot undo the denial of the victim by the rapist. Two wrongs do not make a right. A mature, affirming society will not advocate help that is the opposite of affirmation. Instead, it will affirm the child from the moment of its conception and affirm its mother in her needs. This will include arranging for the child's adoption with good parents who will be glad to do what she herself cannot do, and therefore does not have to do, namely, become a parent to the product of a violent, loveless act she did not choose.

Abortion and the Defective Child

Lastly, the question: Is the possibility or likelihood that the unborn child will be physically or mentally deformed or handicapped ever an indication for abortion?

In a utilitarian philosophy of life concerned with eliminating what is not useful, or a drain on the welfare coffers, or a burden on other citizens, this question cannot but evoke an affirmative answer. The efforts of modern scientists to determine through amniocentesis in the early stages of uterine life the presence of deformities or other abnormalities represent but one example of this utilitarian philosophy. There is little indication that these scientists are aware of the human value of a handicapped child in terms of how it can enhance the humanity of other persons. Some of the truly humane responses evoked by a handicapped child are: a deeper love between his parents as they grow toward one another in their mutual tender concern to make their child's life more joyful; a greater unselfishness of that child's brothers and sisters as they make sacrifices in order to let him participate more fully in their lives; a greater compassion and tenderness on the part of the physicians and other health care personnel trying to bring greater comfort and happiness to that child's life.

Who but the most hardened and selfish individual can deny the significance of a handicapped child as the center and source of man's most precious possession: his unselfish and compassionate love of others? In this extremely utilitarian, and frenziedly busy world, too many affirmed people are frustrated in their desire to give of their love because their fellowmen have turned their backs on them in their frantic pursuit of happiness through self-affirmation. For them the handicapped child is often the only receiver of their affirmation, of the gift of their loving selves. In his dependence and his need for help, the handicapped child can be said to be the preserver of society's most precious, but too neglected, possession; namely, its affectivity.

Too many persons nowadays claim that the defective and handicapped child will never be happy and therefore should be killed before birth. In response to this claim one must ask the question whether science has advanced sufficiently to define and measure the capacity for happiness of even the most severely crippled person. As long as this remains an unknown quantity, who has the right to deny the handicapped the opportunity to experience the happiness of which he might be capable? And is it not true that the handicapped person arouses in those who come to his aid a sense of their own goodness and worth? Thus, a handicapped child contributes in no little way to an increase in the number of affirmed and other-affirming persons, without whom no society can survive. A society made up largely of unaffirmed and self-affirming individuals is doomed to destroy itself through violence in their battles for power and survival.

Abortion and Psychic Suicide

In conclusion, I want to quote the words of the late Protestant theologian, Karl Barth, which fully confirm the insights and conclusions presented in this paper.

> No community, whether family, village, or state, is really strong if it will not carry its weak and even its very weakest members. They belong to it no less than the strong, and the quiet work of their maintenance and care, which might seem useless on a superficial view, is perhaps more effective

than common labor, culture, or historical conflict in knitting it closely and securely together.

On the other hand, a community which regards and trusts its weak members as a hindrance, and even proceeds to their extermination, is on the verge of collapse.[5]

Indeed, a society whose psychic debility has reached the point that it needs to destroy its unborn children, is on the verge of psychic suicide.

Notes

1. *A World Split Apart.*
2. Chodoff, Paul M.D. *Changing Styles in the Neuroses.* 1972 A.P.A. Annual Convention.
3. Terruwe, A. A., M.D., and Baars, C. W., M.D. *Healing the Unaffirmed.* Staten Island, N. Y.: Alba House, 1976.
4. Baars, C. W., M.D. *Born Only Once.* Chicago, IL: Franciscan Herald Press, 1975.
5. Barth, Karl. *Church Dogmatics.* Edinburgh: T&T Clark, 1961. III, No. 4, p. 424.

The Psychological Sequelae of Abortion: Fact and Fallacy

Monte Harris Liebman, M.D.
and
Jolie Siebold Zimmer

Background Information

Although studies differ as to their controls and findings, there has been evidence, though confused at times, to substantiate or suggest the existence of problems related to abortions[4][8][9].

Blumberg et al. report that abortions performed for genetic indications resulted in a higher rate of depression in both the mother (92 percent) and father (86 percent) than reported in other elective abortions. They also noted post-abortion family disharmony and "flashback" phenomenon.[2]

Questionnaire studies have shown that the reactions of post-abortion patients are mixed. Some individuals experience relief and happiness, sometimes along with feelings of guilt, shame, fear, loss, anger, resentment, depression, or remorse.[1] At the same time Kent et al. have findings that suggest the questionnaire data may not reveal the complete picture. Their study of women in psychotherapy indicates that deep pain and bereavement coupled with feelings of love for the unborn are experienced. This reaction would not be perceived or recorded in a questionnaire immediately following abortion, they found, either because of "numbness" as a reaction to the trauma or repression.[6]

Individual clinical studies also reveal significant anxiety and change in marital sexual interests and conduct, moving one author to suggest that abortion did not serve the purpose of mental health.[3]

Spaulding and Cavenar, from an in-depth study of two post-abortion psychotic reactions, reveal that not only did the patients express feelings of guilt and consternation, but in the first case the psychotic reaction occurred on the eve of the anniversary of the abortion and in the second, at the time the girl noted she would have had the baby. The authors conclude by suggesting that physicians may be reluctant to recognize that a "therapeutic" procedure may cause morbidity.[10]

Morbidity is not limited to patients. Personnel, including senior physicians, residents, students, and nurses, have been reported to have untoward reactions which include dread, depression, anxiety, guilt and identity crisis related to the role conflict of healer and abortionist.[5][7]

The factors, fantasies and reactions involved in the abortion problems are many. In our own study our task is four-fold:

1. To document the fact that serious, significant, or disturbing situations have arisen and have been identified through the Pregnancy Aftermath Helpline Counseling Service as abortion-related.

2. To present some of the major complaints and concerns that were expressed from the recordings and notes of the helpline counselors.

3. To discuss various psycho-social and bio-medical factors that seem to influence the choice of abortion and its aftermath.

4. To share some rationale for the approach to helping with the settling of these problems.

Present Study

Materials and Methods

Pregnancy Aftermath Helpline is a free, 24-hour telephone hotline based in Milwaukee, Wisconsin, for people who are having problems or questions following a pregnancy which ends in an abortion, miscarriage, or adoption placement. Its operation began November 1, 1976. Volunteer counselors answer open-ended calls from persons voluntarily contacting the helpline. An anonymous summary data sheet is kept on every call. The data from post-abortion calls have been identified and included in this study.

Findings

From November 1, 1976 to October 1978, 95 post-abortion phone calls were received, 70 from women who stated they had one or more abortions and 25 from persons other than the aborter. Of the 70 women who called following their abortions, 58 expressed a direct relationship between the abortion or abortions and their symptoms of distress.

These 58 calls constitute our sample. The age range of the 31 women who gave their ages was 15-55 years. Twenty-one were between 19 and 25 years (see table).

Age Range of Callers
31 of 58 stated their age

AGE	NUMBER
15	2
16	1
17	1
18	1
19	3
20	6
21	1
22	1
23	5
24	3
25	2
30	1
31	1
36	1
45	1
55	1

Fifty-one of the women stated they had had one abortion; 7 had had two. Three stated the abortions were for medically recommended reasons.

Elapsed Time from Abortion to Call
41 stated elapsed time
3 of these had two abortions

TIME ELAPSED	NUMBER
1 day	2* (a) see below
few days	1
3 days	1* (c)
4 days	1
1 week	5
3 weeks	2
1 month	1
1½ months	1
2 months	1
3 months	1
4 months	2
5 months	2
8 months	1
9 months	1
10 months	2
1 year	2
2 years	4
2½ years	2
3 years	4* (b)
5 years	4
6 years	1
7 years	1
25 years	2

* Two Abortions:
    (a) same woman 1 day and 2 years
    (b) same woman 3 years and 5 years
    (c) same woman few days and 5 years

Forty-one stated the time elapsed since the abortions. Of these, 26 of the abortions had occurred one year or less before the call; 10 of these 26 were one week or less. Sixteen abortions were from 2-7 years before, and 2 were 25 years previous to the call (see table).

The following is a breakdown of the personal, social and psychological sequelae to abortions as reported during the crisis call (see table).

Psychological Sequelae

TYPE OF DISTRESS	NUMBER OF PERSONS
Guilt	22
Anxiety	16
Depression	15
Sense of Loss	11
Anger	11
Change in Relationship with Boyfriend	11
Crying	11
Feeling Misled by Misinformation or Lack of Information	10
Deterioration of Self Image	7
Regret or Remorse	7
Nightmares	7
Anxiety about Possible Infertility	7
Loneliness/Alienation	6
Marital Problems	6
Physical Concerns	5
Surprise at Emotional Reaction	4
Disturbance in Sleep Patterns	4
Phantom Child	3
Flashbacks	2
Likely Psychotic Reactions	2
Hopelessness	2
Helplessness	1
Powerlessness	1
Change in Friendship (other than boyfriend)	1

Guilt: Guilt over the abortion was the most common reaction, reported by 22 women. They have stated that they "murdered a baby," "did something very wrong," "didn't do what a good mother would have done." One woman had "hang-ups and guilt" over an abortion 25 years ago. Those who mentioned God expressed two ideas. Some believe God forgave them but they can't forgive themselves. Others think God is punishing them through the emotional trauma they are experiencing or through subsequent miscarriage. One woman wanted to get pregnant immediately after the abortion, but said, "I should never have a child because I can't undo this abortion."

Anxiety: Sixteen women expressed a sense of apprehension and anxiety in the post-abortion period. At least two said they were "going crazy." One said she was "fearful." Another wanted "to get in a car and drive and drive and get out and start life over again."

Depression: Fifteen women defined their emotional state as "depression" or described symptoms of it. Some feel completely immobilized. "I can't get myself to do anything," and "I can't get interested in anyone or anything since the abortion," are statements that have been made. Three women reported they were missing days of work because of their emotional state. One woman compared her present state to her depression after her husband died: "This is worse and there is no end to it."

Sense of Loss: Eleven women articulated their loss over the baby-who-will-never-be. "This is the family I would have had," one woman said. Women who feel this loss have described a number of reactions: they cannot look at babies, little children or pregnant women; they are jealous of mothers. Some have said they want to get pregnant again to replace the lost child; one wanted to take in foster children. Although not counted in this category, sense of loss sometimes extends beyond the lost child. Some women are simultaneously experiencing loss of their sexual partner or husband if the desired relationship has deteriorated (see Change in Relationship with Boyfriend and Change in Relationship with Husband). At least two women expressed loss regarding values they once had that were obliterated by the abortion (see Change in Self Image).

Anger: Eleven women expressed anger toward variously involved persons: abortion clinic counselors "who didn't give the other side of the picture," didn't warn the woman of possible emotional problems, or didn't make the woman "stop and think"; at boyfriends and spouses for not supporting them when they needed help. For instance, one woman was angry at her husband for forcing her to have an abortion "for financial reasons."

Change in Relationship with Boyfriend: Eleven women reported a change in their relationships with their boyfriends, all but one of them for the worse. Five of these were distressed and confused that their boyfriends had abandoned them after their abortions. One woman and man—the caller described their relationship as "long and stable"—decided on the abortion together. She asked him to pick her up from the hospital and he said no; she has seen him once in the three weeks since the abortion. Another woman said her boyfriend gave her the money for the abortion and she "hasn't seen him since." Of this category 4 felt their boyfriends were not concerned about their emotional distress after the abortion. One man told the woman to "grow up" when she tried to talk about it. One case also was reported in which the boyfriend got angry when he found out about the abortion and refused to speak to the woman. In these 10 cases, then, the women felt their relationships had deteriorated since the abortion. One woman said her relationship with her boyfriend was no longer sexual, but did not make a value statement about the change.

Crying: Eleven women either cried during the phone call or reported they had been crying since the abortion. Some have said, "I cried all night," "I cried all day," "I cried for two days" before making the call, or simply, "I cry all the time."

Feel Misled by Misinformation or Lack of Information: Ten women felt misled by persons they went to for help after the abortion. Five of them felt they were given misinformation. Women were told their pregnancy was "like a fish," "like an acorn," or "only tissue." When one woman voiced her concern at the clinic that the abortion might be killing, the counselor said, "Don't think of it as killing. Think of it as taking blood out of your uterus to get your periods going again." When another called the clinic after the abortion to discuss her post-abortion emotional distress, she was told "only 2 percent of the women feel like this." Five in this category verbalized their dismay at the lack of information they were given. Women said they were upset because they were not informed of the possibility of miscarriage, of sterility, or of post-abortion emotions. In addition, 2 of them were resentful that they were not given alternatives.

Deterioration of Self Image: Seven women stated that their views of themselves have been lower since their abortions. They described themselves now as "a bad person," "not worthy to be loved or have any more children," or "violent." The last woman was especially upset because she had always viewed herself as a sort of pacifist, against any violence including that on television, and ready to be protective "when little puppies are hurt." Another felt the abortion had "castrated" her, leaving her with the feeling she was asexual and like an "amputee."

At least two women said they were disappointed in themselves and viewed the abortion as going against their previously held values or "copping out." One caller identified her problem as reconciling her former pro-life views and her abortion. "After an abortion," another said, "you're never the same."

Regret/Remorse: Seven women expressed regret over the abortion. "I am so sorry I did it," one woman said. The finality of the abortion has upset some. "I can never get my baby back." "I can never undo it." Self-recrimination and the statement, "But I had no choice," have sometimes followed such comments.

Anxiety Over Possible Infertility: Seven women have worried that they may never have another child. In some cases there are no symptoms of physical problems; in other cases there are. One woman was afraid she was sterile because she hemorrhaged three months after her abortion. Two others were concerned that an earlier abortion caused them to miscarry. One of these attributes two tubal pregnancies to her previous abortion. Another, now in a relationship with a man who had a vasectomy, is beginning to think she may never have another child.

Nightmares: Seven women said they were having nightmares after their abortions.

Feeling of Loneliness or Alienation: Six women felt bound to their reaction and separated from those around them. Some felt they had no one to confide in.

Marital Problems: Six women described problems or changes in their marriages after their abortions. One husband blamed the woman for her inability to conceive since her abortion seven years earlier. Some reported that their husbands lacked concern about their emotional distress. Sexual dimensions were present in three of these cases. One woman, for instance, did not want to have sex since her abortion and was "practically raped" by her husband.

Physical Concerns: Five women called regarding physical concerns. For example, one was worried about bloating and clotting after her abortion, another about abnormal results of a pap test, and another, now pregnant, about whether to inform her doctor of her abortion.

Surprise at Emotional Reaction: Four women were surprised and dismayed at the intensity and duration of their reactions even though one felt relieved immediately after the procedure. They asked: "Do other people have these same problems?" "Is my emotional pain normal?" "Why didn't anyone tell me I'd freak out?" No woman of the 58 reported that she was informed of any possible psychological after-effects of the abortion.

Disturbances of Sleeping Patterns: Four women have experienced insomnia.

Phantom Child: The "phantom child" phenomenon occurs when a person imagines her aborted child as old as it would be had it not been aborted. Three women have described this reaction. One reported unsettling, recurrent dreams (counted in Nightmares) of a little boy the age her child would have been. The second reported seeing "her babies" whenever she sees other children the ages they would have been, and the third described in detail the age and appearance of "her daughter."

Flashbacks: Two women reported having flashbacks of the abortion procedure, one after six years.

Psychotic Reactions: Two women's beliefs did not coincide with likely reality. After three years one woman still believed her aborted fetus to be alive and another felt that "everyone was the devil."

Hopelessness: Two women expressed the feeling that they could see no way out of their depressions.

Helplessness: One woman felt overwhelmed and unable to cope with her emotional reactions. This same woman expressed feelings of hopelessness.

Powerlessness: One woman was angry with her doctor, feeling as though she were a "victim."

Change in Friends: One woman noted a change in a friend after her abortion. Following the abortion her roommate moved out. "She threw abortion in my face."

The following information was also given although it does not constitute sequelae of abortion. Seven women said that they felt they were threatened or pressured into the abortion by husbands, boyfriends, or parents. Five said they were not stopped during their decision-making process before their abortions. Five felt a lack of concern on the part of abortion personnel.

Of the 25 persons other than the aborter who called there were 9 mothers, 5 friends, 4 boyfriends, 3 husbands, 2 sisters, and 2 other persons.

Three of these calls did not relate directly to any untoward post-abortion reaction in the caller. These three callers were a doctor's office assistant, a husband, and a boyfriend-father who were respectively seeking information regarding the handling of a post-abortion problem, genetic counseling regarding mongolism, and family advice regarding the children.

Of the remaining 22 reactors, 7 expressed concern about the aborter. This varied from what effect an abortion would have on a

Abortion Related Calls from Others
25 calls received

By matching the letters the reader will be able to identify the caller with the reported distress.

NUMBER	CALLER (Significant Other)	
9	Mother	D F H I J K M N P
5	Friend	A L O R V
4	Boyfriend	B G Q U
2	Husband	E T
2	Sister	C S
22	Total	

DISTRESSES

7	Concerned about aborter	C L M O R S V
6	Guilt	A E I K N T
5	Discord: Social/Familial	B F J Q U
2	Anxiety	D G
1	Depression	H
1	Post-abortion Bleeding	P
22	Total	

son who was presently taking his girlfriend for one, to the search for help for a post-abortion suicidal sister.

Guilty feelings were expressed by 5 callers. One husband, who stated he thought he need not concern himself with the social and cultural factors concerning abortion, felt guilty about his lack of concern and involvement when he learned his wife had an abortion without his knowledge. Two hours after taking a daughter to a hospital for an abortion, one mother began experiencing guilt and ambivalence, stating, "That was my grandchild. . . . This is a baby that will never be born." They had felt they could not give up the child through adoption before the abortion. One mother felt guilty about "agreeing" to an abortion and one friend felt guilty for letting a friend have one. A husband whose wife had two abortions and a recent miscarriage was beginning to feel guilty. (He reported his wife as experiencing loss, guilt, and depression.) One mother called concerned and feeling guilty about the death of her daughter who died of a respiratory ailment one week following an abortion. She felt she had contributed to it by allowing the abortion.

Five calls related **discord** between father and daughter, parents, friends, boyfriend and aborter. In two cases the daughter was "kicked out."

One mother was **anxious** about her daughter's "thrashing," anger, and depression since the abortion. A boyfriend called, wanting to stop his girlfriend from getting one.

Depression, experienced by one mother, was related to concern about the daughter's untoward reactions. The mother had become immobilized.

Post-abortion bleeding was the reason for another mother's involvement and search for adequate medical attention.

Conclusion

In the cases studied, it was found that women experienced varied reactions to their abortions that were both immediate and long-term. These sequelae have threatened the woman's view of herself, her relationships, and her future as well as her emotional stability and well being, and have impaired her ability to cope effectively with the present. Calls from relatives and friends of the aborters indicate that the aftermath of abortions significantly extends beyond the intrapersonal and touches the interpersonal dimension of life.

Our study represents actual identifiable reactions of helpline callers, the immediate factors with which the individuals are struggling. Although not noted before, many of the callers were in immediate states of crisis and desperation. Not infrequently, referrals are made to other community resources. The counselors listen with calm and non-judgmental attitudes and attempt to define with the caller the immediate reason for the call, helping the caller to formulate and follow an immediate plan for resolution and/or continuing help with other agencies and persons.

Our experience has made us acutely aware of the need for more accurate information regarding the conditions of abortion.

What is apparent from all our information and that of others is that people are not well-informed or prepared for the serious problems and decisions that sexual behavior and abortion create.

References

1. Adler, Nancy E. Emotional Responses of Women Following Therapeutic Abortion. *American Journal of Orthopsychiatry.* 5: (1975), 446-454.

2. Blumberg, Bruce; Golbus, Mitchell; Hanson, Karl. The Psychological Sequelae of Abortion Performed for Genetic Indication. *American Journal of Obstetrics and Gynecology.* 22 (1975).

3. Calef, Victor. The Hostility of Parents to Children: Some Notes on Infertility, Child Abuse, and Abortions. *International Journal of Psychoanalytic Psychotherapy.* 1: (1972), 79-96.

4. Elkins, Mary. Psychiatric Complications of Abortion. Unpublished Review of Literature, 1977.

5. Kane, Francis J.; Feldman, Michael; Jain, Susheila; Lipton, Morris A. Emotional Reactions on Abortion Services Personnel. *Archives of General Psychiatry.* 28: (1973), 409-411.

6. Kent, Ian; Greenwood, R. C.; Nicholls, W.; Loeken, Janice. Emotional Sequelae of Therapeutic Abortion: A Comparative Study. Presented at the annual meeting of the Canadian Psychiatric Association, 1978.

7. Rosen, Norma. Between Guilt and Gratification: Abortion Doctors Reveal Their Feelings. *New York Times Magazine,* April 17, 1977.

8. Simon, N. and Senturia, A. Psychiatric Sequelae of Therapeutic Abortion: A Review of the Literature, 1935-1964. *Archives of General Psychiatry.* 15: (1966), 378-389.

9. Simon, Nathan; Senturia, Audrey; Rothman, David: Psychiatric Illness Following Therapeutic Abortion. *American Journal of Psychiatry.* 124: (1967), 59-65.

10. Spaulding, Jean G.; Cavenar, Jesse O., Jr.; Psychoses Following Therapeutic Abortion. *American Journal of Psychiatry.* 135: (1978), 364-365.

Abortion and the Cognitive Foundation of Dehumanization

by David Mall

The psychopathology of abortion transcends the narrow parameters of the purely emotional. That this psychopathology may have a cognitive foundation is amply illustrated in the language used to describe the object to be aborted. It is generally conceded by those participating most actively in the abortion debate that this language serves either to humanize or dehumanize the unborn entity.

Beyond the intriguing possible connection between language and worldview as suggested by Benjamin Whorf lies the largely uninvestigated realm of epistemology. Beyond even the emerging movement in psychiatry which is attempting to focus attention on cognitive defects,[1] there seems to be a still deeper stratum of how we come to know the very concepts we debate. In the writer's judgment, the question of abortion has deep epistemological significance, a significance which can be seen and amplified in the work of Jean Piaget.

What follows is a brief outline of the epistemology of abortion. It is a sketch in Piagetian terms of what may be at stake cognitively in analyzing the definitional requirements of our humanity. This preliminary assessment is by no means definitive, although the technique itself may have application to other questions which hinge upon what it means to be human. It is intended to be suggestive to philosophers and rhetoricians who are concerned about the intellectual foundations of social action.

Abortion is a question which involves two aspects of mental functioning: How one views or relates to 1) the physical world and 2) the moral or social world. These aspects are the world of objects (What is it? Is it human?) and the world of subjects (What should we do with it? Should we abort it?). Although, strictly speaking, they are operationally inseparable and their reciprocal interaction is not clearly understood,[2] for purposes of this analysis we will focus upon the physical aspect and let the moral aspect assume a background position.[3]

There is a great divergence of thought about when human life begins. Seven justices of the U.S. Supreme Court claimed complete ignorance of the matter in their *Roe* v. *Wade* decision. "We need not resolve the difficult question of when life begins," they said. "When those trained in the respective disciplines of medicine, philosophy, and theology are unable to arrive at any consensus, the judiciary, at this point in the development of man's knowledge, is not in a position to speculate as to the answer." The justices then proceeded "to note briefly the wide divergence of thinking on this most sensitive and difficult question," and considered the standard and contradictory responses from conception to natural birth.[4]

By notable contrast, the Federal Constitutional Court of West Germany took a different view of when human life begins. In construing the meaning of the Basic Law provision that "Everyone has a right to life . . . ," the German court said:

> Life in the sense of historical existence of a human individual, exists according to definite biological-physiological knowledge, in any case from the 14th day after conception (nidation, individuation). . . .
>
> The process of development which has begun at that point is a continuing process which exhibits no sharp demarcation and does not allow a precise division of the various steps of development of the human life. . . .
>
> The right to life is guaranteed to everyone who "lives"; no distinction can be made between various stages of the life developing itself before birth, or between unborn and born life.[5]

The key contrasting definitional elements in the biological reasoning of the two opinions, it would appear, is continuous as opposed to discontinuous development. This should become clearer as we proceed with the analysis.

The divergence of thought about abortion seen in the contrasting judgments of two respected supreme courts represents world society's collective mental disequilibrium. It is our species' failure to test reality in a consistent manner and reflects an inability to process cognitive information properly. The writer contends that embedded in the thinking of the U.S. Supreme Court is a cognitive error with clear indications of irrationality. The key question then becomes: How could it happen? What follows may provide an inkling of an answer.

Piagetian Epistemology

Epistemology was once considered an integral part of the study of philosophy, but contemporary scholarship has given it an independent status with specific laws governing its behavior and understanding. Logic, aesthetics, and ethics have not yet achieved a similar status and are still considered a part of philosophy as originally conceived by the Greeks. Experimental psychology, on the other hand, has also become dissociated from natural philosophy, as has political science from political philosophy. Today, along with epistemology, they show their kinship to philosophy by being amenable to the general rules of metaphysics.

By definition, epistemology is the study of valid knowledge or how humans can reliably know what they know. Its older philosophical aspect was formalist and static while its newer scientific aspect is genetic and dynamic. This scientific aspect is tied to cognitive psychology, particularly the developmental psychology of Jean Piaget, which is clearly process oriented.

Piaget's major contribution to human knowledge—or at least what he wishes to be known by—is what he has called genetic epistemology, a phrase he coined. What this term implies is that knowledge has a psychogenesis or is continuously constructed through an individual's interaction with the environment. In Piaget's work in child psychology, his theory of knowledge becomes essentially a theory of adapting thoughts to reality. "[G]enetic psychology consists of using child psychology to find the solution of general psychological problems."[6]

Literally, genetic epistemology is a term which means a knowing which becomes incrementally more accurate. It studies the process of getting from lower to higher levels of awareness or lesser to greater levels of validity. This, according to Piaget, is fundamentally a scientific or factual question. We come to know the physical world through stages of progressive comprehension.

Number and space, time and speed, chance and causality are epistemological categories which Piaget and his collaborators over a period of some fifty years have studied. Every person's comprehension of these categories is by degrees or by transformations obeying certain laws which have been discovered and are demonstrable. Each human being from the very earliest period of development grasps them by invariant sequence. Piaget's child psychology then, becomes "a kind of mental embryology."[7] As the human conceptus goes through certain stages of development, so does the human mind.

Within Piaget's developmental theory there are several key notions which bear upon the abortion question as embodied in the problem of when life begins. Two of these notions are central: object conservation and object permanence. Both will be considered in detail.

Object Conservation

In what the writer considers to be a remarkable statement, Piaget and his collaborator Szeminska once asserted that "conservation constitutes a necessary condition for all rational activity." They did not claim that it is sufficient to account for all such activity, nor did they claim that it "exhausts the representation of reality or the dynamism of the intellectual processes." Their only claim was that conservation is "a necessary condition of all experience and all reasoning."[8] The writer will contend that this notion applies directly to the problem of when life begins and, conversely, when life ceases to be.

Piaget's classic experiments with continuous and discontinuous quantities will help explain the notion of conservation.

Continuous Quantity. A small child under the age of six is given two glasses (A and B) of equal size and each filled to the same level with a liquid. The contents of one are then poured into two smaller glasses (C and D) each to the same level. The child is then asked whether the two smaller glasses are equal to B. If the child is unable to conserve, the quantity of liquid either diminishes or increases according to the number or size of the containers. Perceptually captivated by a single parameter, the child thinks that there has been an actual change in the quantity of liquid.[9]

Discontinuous Quantity. The same small child is given two equal sets of beads (red and green). They can be put in separate containers as before or a necklace can be made of one. The test of conservation occurs when the beads are evaluated separately or when massed. If a necklace is made from one set of beads, the child may think that it will not be the same length as the other set. Again, as previously in the quantity of liquid, there is thought to be an actual change in the number of beads. With the use of beads, however, each unit can be used to measure one-to-one correspondence, which is an origin of the concept of number.[10]

Whether or not humanity exists in prenatal children is analogically similar to the conservation of continuous and discontinuous substances. The dramatic periods of birth, viability, quickening, or implantation, or the presence of heartbeat or brain waves can be considered perceptual captivations which can distract a contemplator's judgment so that the humanity ceases to be conserved. The humanity which exists after the new biological event fails to exist before it. Just as in the Piagetian sense a change in the size or shape of the container does not change the quantity of the contents, so the hiatuses of intrauterine development do not add to or detract from the unborn's humanity. No biological modification can change its genetic and therefore characteristic constancy.

The writer contends that the notion of conservation can indeed be generalized to the question of the unborn's humanity. An individual's humanity is an inherent property of the object in the phenomenon of pregnancy known as a fertilized ovum, blastocyst, fetus, or whatever. If humanity were not an inherent property from the very beginning, there would be no way to harmonize the entire system with its functioning elements. To assign humanity to a particular developmental hiatus is to disrupt the natural pattern of constancies to which the mind normally adheres in comprehending the physical world.

When the cognitive process is dominated by perception, it is said to be stimulus bound. This is not a failure of perception so much as it is a failure of the intelligence to function properly in achieving an equilibrium between whole and parts. Since, in the Piagetian sense, perception is incomplete cognition, it tends to emphasize whole over parts or parts over whole. Intelligence equates the two as in the conservation examples previously cited. The liquid in glasses C and D (parts) are said to be more or less than the liquid in glass B (whole). The beads when strung out (parts) are said to be more or fewer than when massed (whole).

Contemplating the human offspring *in utero* brings the Piagetian notion of conservation into full play. To concentrate on fetal heartbeat or brainwave in assigning humanity to the unborn is to concentrate on the part and neglect the whole. And to exclaim as some abortionists do in contemplating the conceptus, "But it's so tiny!", is to concentrate on the whole and neglect the parts. Clearly, the error is cognitive in failing to conserve the balance between parts and whole or a system and its elements.

Children's literature is often illustrative of Piagetian epistemology. One such story, applicable to the abortion debate and to the notion of conservation, is *Horton Hears a Who* by Dr. Seuss. This delightful story contains a subtle lesson for all who are beguiled by mere appearances. It is a classic example of how the conception of size can dominate our thinking.

Horton, the elephant, while bathing in a jungle pool, hears a tiny yelp from a speck of dust blowing by in the air. Although the sound comes from someone too small to be seen, Horton believes it is his duty to help.

[S]ome poor little person who's shaking with fear

> That he'll blow in the pool! He has no way to steer!
> I'll just have to save him. Because, after all,
> A person's a person, no matter how small.

The last sentence becomes a sort of refrain indicating the story's central idea.

The rest of the story involves Horton's kindhearted attempts to allay the skepticism and suspicion of his fellow animals, including a mother and baby kangaroo and a group of monkeys known as the Wickersham Brothers. The latter are such scoffers that they threaten to harm what they cannot see or hear, the tiny inhabitants of the speck of dust living in a town called Whoville. A monkey finally snatches the clover on which the speck of dust resides and gives it to an eagle named Vlad Vlad-i-koff, who later drops it in an enormous patch of clover. After Horton searches for and finds the right clover, the story builds to a climax with the skeptical animals attempting to boil the speck of dust in a Beezle-Nut stew.

The inhabitants of Whoville are alerted to their plight by the mayor, who exhorts them all to make as much noise as possible in order to be heard by the animals. The whole town cooperates except one small Who named Jo-Jo, who is discovered by the mayor playing with a yo-yo in the Fairfax Apartments, Apt. 12-J. With the battle for Whoville all but lost, Jo-Jo and the mayor climb to the top of the Eiffelberg Tower, where Jo-Jo's voice is added to all the others in one last effort. The story ends with the Whos finally being heard. "And then their whole world was saved by the Smallest of All!"

Obviously, this is an allegory about the importance of smallness. Yet, without any imagination, it is also a sound lesson in the epistemology of abortion. Horton, who has sensitive large ears, represents the inner ear of science which is not confused by mere appearance. The whole is a whole no matter how small, if all the essential parts are there. A fertilized ovum, a blastocyst, or an embryo, as a completely integrated system, is like the town of Whoville. In the Dr. Seuss story, the scoffers are overwhelmed by size. What they cannot see, cannot be human, a likely refrain from the skeptics of every age, including the ardent abortionists of today.

According to the *Roe* v. *Wade* decision, viability becomes the minimum criterion for the conferring of humanity or personhood. "With respect to the State's important and legitimate interest in potential life," the justices said, "the 'compelling' point is at viability."[11] Although the court's opinion also includes another gestational point of focus which is obviously birth, this two-tiered focusing is equivalent to the preoperational thinking of children. During the preoperational period of development, the child can only focus on a single aspect of an object, an incapacity called "centering." The child defines the object in relation to its dominant function or compelling feature, a clear indication of immature reasoning.

The irrational centering upon viability in pro-abortion thinking has a parallel in the children's story of *Winnie-the-Pooh*. Eeyore, the donkey, like the unborn child, is victimized by centering. Those familiar with the story will remember that Eeyore loses his tail which Pooh promises to help find and which Owl obviously considers to be the donkey's most compelling feature. While visiting Owl, Pooh sees a similarity between the bell-rope over Owl's door and Eeyore's tail.

> "Handsome bell-rope, isn't it?" said Owl. Pooh nodded. "It reminds me of something," he said,. "but I can't think what. Where did you get it?"

Owl then describes how he came to hang it from his door. When he first saw it hanging from a bush, he rang it thinking someone must be living in the bush. Nothing happened, however, and when he pulled it again it came off in his hand. Owl then took the bell-rope home, since apparently nobody wanted it. A tail without a donkey is not a tail; hang it from a door and it becomes a bell-rope.[12]

Similarly, in pro-abortion thinking and in the thinking of the U.S. Supreme Court, real infants cannot be attached to mothers except under certain circumstances. When they are so attached at a nonviable stage of development they become something else. Just as Pooh in looking at Eeyore's detached tail in the functional guise of a bell-rope thought it reminded him of something, so also if one were to see an unborn child just before viability it would more than likely remind one of something—a child.

The concept of viability is governed by circumstance. A child is just as helpless before as after birth. Such a simple demonstrable fact should be compelling to any sufficiently unencumbered rational mind able to understand the rudiments of intrauterine growth. Babies born at term and left unattended for very long will die. And if, as in the *Winnie-the-Pooh* story, a tail does not have to wag to be a tail, then perhaps a baby does not have to be viable to be a baby.[13]

Object Permanence

An even more fundamental central notion than conservation is that of object permanence. Before a property of an object can be conserved, the object itself must be considered permanent. As Piaget puts it, "The permanence of the object . . . constitutes the very first of those fundamental ideas of conservation."[14]

The classic examples of failing to attain object permanence are that of 1) the neonate who loses a nursing bottle under the crib covers and when it becomes visible again but with the bottom up, does not consider it the same object, and of 2) the baby under six months who is playing with a small object like an empty match box which is then taken away and in full view placed under a handkerchief.

> He thus behaves as though the object were absorbed by the cloth and ceased to exist at the very moment that it left the perceptual field; or else, and this amounts to the same thing, he possesses no behavior enabling him to search for the object which has disappeared whether by action (lifting the screen) or by thought (imagining).[15]

In this latter example, the child immediately loses interest in the object insofar as there is no attempt to remove the cover to retrieve it. For such children, objects simply vanish once they have departed the perceptual field.

The adult in contemplating the offspring *in utero* and imagining it nonhuman commits the same type of cognitive error. A good way of exposing this error is by reversing the developmental process. In the writer's experience, most who are uncertain about the presence of the unborn's humanity will grant that it is human at birth and immediately before birth. Moving the development back to viability then presents a test for our theory. For the abortionist of strong conviction, humanity exists after viability but not before. Nonviability' is thus equivalent to the covering placed over a child's object as in the nursing bottle or match box examples noted previously. The child literally disappears. The humanity it possessed after viability is there no longer. And the same holds true for other developmental stages all the way back to conception or fertilization. The object as an intuitively recognizable human being ceases to exist.

Efforts by the abortionist to make the unborn baby disappear (subconsciously, of course) can be seen in the language often used in the abortion debate to describe this unborn entity—"a blob, piece of tissue, or clump of cells." Such language is akin to the primitive incantation of the sorcerer wishing to do his victim harm. They are verbal attempts to dehumanize or to think out of existence. In anthropological terms this is the use of magic; in epistemological terms, the denial of permanency to a portion of the physical world. If we looked at the rest of the physical world like the U.S. Supreme Court wishes us to look at intrauterine life, we would be living in Alice's Wonderland, where words lose their meaning and solipsism reigns supreme.

Epistemology and psychotherapy are brought into convergence with the Piagetian notion of egocentrism. From the epistemological viewpoint, egocentrism is an attitude which Piaget describes as opposed to objectivity and as "confusion of the ego and the external world." He considers it essentially "an inability to differentiate between the ego and the social environment," whereby what appears to perception becomes the sole reality.[16] From the psychotherapeutic viewpoint, egocentrism is a basic problem in reality testing which can ultimately render the patient incapable of engaging in harmonious interpersonal relations. Piaget claims that it "persists throughout life during periods of mental inertia."[17]

The person who argues that because a woman has a right to control her own body she also has a right to abortion-on-demand is confused about subject-object differentiation. Pregnancy becomes detached from the psychological self, and the pregnant woman's attitudes toward it exhibit an incomplete separation-individuation with all the attending psychological problems. The woman who cannot conceive of the fetus as separate from herself is enmeshed in an egocentrism which falsifies fundamental logical relationships between self and others and ultimately distorts the object itself. This distortion, as noted before, can be seen in the dehumanizing language often used to describe the unborn child. And ironically, women who at one time in history were considered the chattel property of men are now being asked to relate to their unborn offspring in a similiar fashion.

A sense of the other, a stable sense of the separate existence of physical objects (babies) even when they are outside one's immediate perceptual field (in the womb),is a mark of epistemological exactitude. Such an equilibrium of thought conforming to reality is a characteristic of truth as it pertains to the physical world. Insofar as abortion represents a broad failure to distinguish between aspects of the self and aspects of the external world, it contributes to one's inability to take the viewpoint of others in social situations. This failure is sometimes reflected in pathological conditions and in the tendency to generalize the lethality of abortion to other areas of social concern; i.e., capital punishment, war, etc. At the very minimum it represents a misuse of cognitive functioning.

A way out of the serious epistemological problem posed by abortion is to consider the human being at all stages of development as an open system. It can be demonstrated, for example, that each human person from conception onward represents a unique genetic package which is integrated, grows, metabolizes, and responds to stimuli—a biological unit never to be repeated in the history of the cosmos. To the argumentative layman these are undisputed signs of life; to the rational scientific reasoner they are also the facts of life. Most life scientists believe that human life begins at conception. To think otherwise would lack epistemological rigor and do violence to the great cognitive tool of science, causal reasoning.

It is hard for society to face its own irrationality. Over the centuries science in general and biomedicine in particular have provided a rich breeding ground for cognitive error. Bloodletting was once an accepted medical treatment but is now considered retrograde. The earth was once considered flat and also the center of the universe. Throughout history, from witch-burning that killed Joan of Arc to Lysenkoism that crippled Soviet agriculture, bad rules have been made by mistake. The pseudoscience of astrology still finds millions of believers in highly industrialized countries. And the U.S. government continues to subsidize the growing of cigarette tobacco, while the U.S. Surgeon General publicly declares it injurious to health.

Cognitive functioning should reflect the real world. Structures of the human mind, in their evolutionary development, should reflect structures of the physical world that are actually true. When man willingly accepts a false structure, or one that is reluctantly imposed upon him by society, he is likely to behave irrationally. His failure to affirm life, which all of nature beckons him not to do, results in the destruction of his offspring through abortion.

It would appear, therefore, that a strong case can be made for the fact that the psychiatric sequelae of induced abortion is the result of the painful turmoil in one's psychic life brought about, in part, by some false conceptions about the physical world. This analysis, of course, is meant to oversimplify. The epistemology, however, is sound. The psychic debilities of abortion, now beginning to be reported in the scientific literature, flow from the unwarranted dehumanization of one's offspring, a grotesque example of irrationality.

That the unborn are not human is an old wives' tale. It is exactly what one would expect from a world in which so many things are judged solely by appearance. "But it doesn't look human" is the perfect observation to emanate from what Nobel Laureate Charles B. Huggins calls "The Age of the Shoddy." It is the perfect mentality to forge pseudoscience into social policy. To consider the dynamic system of prenatal human life to be anything but human is to assume a naive view of the physical world.

The abortion controversy is a classic encounter between folk thinking and scientific thinking. As Boulding, who coined this richly descriptive duality, would say, "Folk man sees the world in an illusory perspective."[18] Where there is chaos he sees order and where order, chaos. Appearances easily deceive him. He fails (or refuses) to detect order in the earliest stages of intrauterine development. His failure (or refusal) is ratified by the act of abortion.

The real tragedy of folk thinking is that, if engaged in for any length of time, it begins to erode the data base, that basic deposit of information about the physical and social worlds. One false reaction to mere appearance can lead to others. If an unborn child is not human or a person in "the whole sense,"[19] then what is? What appearance must authentic humanity assume? What about the terminally ill or severely handicapped? These are some of the general and specific questions which folk thinking and the pressures for social progress will inevitably provoke.

Scientific man, on the other hand, realizing that true knowledge is often accompanied by ignorance, strives with great effort to suspend his innate egocentrism to get a clearer view of reality. Like Copernicus before him, who shattered forever an outmoded egocentric view of the cosmos, scientific man engages reality in a rigorous testing of causal reasoning. He agrees with Antoine de Saint-Exupéry that "what is essential is invisible to the eye." He views man as a system related to other systems which are in a constant state of becoming. He fights a relentless struggle against the superstition and naive determinism of folk thinking.

Keenly aware that error is often bound up with truth and evil with good, scientific man suspends judgment until more facts are in. Where possible, he corrects evil, pursues truth, and refuses to live with irrationality. He wages a long and painful struggle, but the result is ultimately a world closer to the ideal of justice and truth.

Notes

1. For a scholarly statement of this new movement, see George Serban, ed., *Cognitive Defects in the Development of Mental Illness* (New York: Bruner/Mazel, 1978).

2. Some of this reciprocal interaction can be seen in the titles and content of two books on the abortion question. Note especially Linda Bird Francke, *The Ambivalence of Abortion* (New York: Random House, 1978); and Robert E. Cooke, An-

dre E. Hellegers, Robert G. Hoyt, and Herbert W. Richardson, eds., *The Terrible Choice: The Abortion Dilemma* (New York: Bantam Books, Inc., 1968).

3. Using a framework devised by Lawrence Kohlberg and his associates at Harvard, the writer has analyzed the moral (socio-emotional) aspect of abortion in a forthcoming book to be published in the summer of 1979.

4. *Roe* v. *Wade*, 410 U.S. 113, 159 (1973).

5. Robert E. Jonas and John D. Gorby, "West German Abortion Decision: A Contrast to *Roe* v. *Wade*," *The John Marshall Journal of Practice and Procedure*, IX, No. 3 (Spring, 1976), p. 638.

6. Jean Piaget, *Psychology and Epistemology*, trans. by Arnold Rosin (New York: The Viking Press, 1971), p. 45. For those unfamiliar with Piaget's epistemology, see Jean Piaget, *Genetic Epistemology*, trans. by Eleanor Duckworth (New York: Columbia University Press, 1970); and Jean Piaget, *The Principles of Genetic Epistemology*, trans. by Wolfe Mays (New York: Basic Books, Inc., 1972).

7. *Ibid.*, p. 24.

8. Jean Piaget, *The Child's Conception of Number* (New York: W. W. Norton and Co., 1965), p. 3.

9. *Ibid.*, pp. 3-24.

10. *Ibid.*, pp. 25-38.

11. 410 U.S. 113, 163 (1973).

12. I am indebted to Dorothy G. Singer and Tracey A. Revenson for reminding me of this episode in A. A. Milne's work. See Dorothy G. Singer and Tracey A. Revenson, *A Piaget Primer: How a Child Thinks* (New York: International Universities Press, Inc., 1978), p. 37.

13. One of the great centerings of all time is, of course, related to the white man's conception of blacks. The latter were held in bondage for centuries because man focused on the nonessential characteristic of color. John Calhoun even carried his centering one step further: "Show me a nigger," he said, "who can do a problem in Euclid or parse a Greek verb and I'll admit he's a human being." Quoted in Martin Gardner, *Fads and Fallacies in the Name of Science* (New York: Dover Publications, Inc., 1957), p.156.

14. Jean Piaget, *The Psychology of Intelligence*, trans. by Malcolm Piercy and D. E. Berlyne (Totowa, New Jersey: Littlefield, Adams and Co., 1966), p. 108.

15. *Ibid.*, p. 109.

16. Jean Piaget, *The Moral Judgment of the Child*, trans. by Marjorie Gabain (New York: The Free Press, 1965), p. 93.

17. Jean Piaget, *The Language and Thought of the Child*, trans. by Margorie Gabain and Ruth Gabain (New York: The Humanities Press, Inc., 1959), p. 271.

18. Kenneth E. Boulding, *The Meaning of the Twentieth Century* (New York: Harper and Row, 1964), p. 67.

19. 410 U.S. 113, 162 (1973).

Editors and Authors

David Mall
Author, editor, teacher.

Walter F. Watts, M.D., F.A.C.O.G.
Clinical Professor, Department of Obstetrics and Gynecology, Stritch School of Medicine, Loyola University.

Conrad W. Baars, M.D.
Psychiatrist (San Antonio). Education: Oxford University, Delft University, University of Amsterdam. Publications: Author of numerous books and articles.

Andrew Feldmar, Ph.D.
Clinical Psychologist (Vancouver). Education: University of Toronto, University of Western Ontario, Simon Fraser University. Publications: Author of numerous articles.

Howard W. Fisher, M.D.
Psychiatrist (Minneapolis). Education: University of Minnesota. Faculty Appointments: University of Minnesota Hospitals. Publications: Author of numerous articles.

Monte H. Liebman, M.D.
Psychiatrist (Milwaukee). Education: University of Wisconsin. Faculty Appointments: Medical College of Wisconsin. Publications: Author of numerous articles.

Sandra K. Mahkorn, M.S.
Medical Student, University of Wisconsin; Former Counselor, Witness Support Anti-Rape Unit, District Attorney's Office, Milwaukee County, Wisconsin. Education: University of Wisconsin (Milwaukee). Faculty Appointments: Milwaukee School of the Arts.

George E. Maloof, M.D.
Psychiatrist (San Francisco). Education: Harvard University, Georgetown University. Publications: Author of numerous articles.

Robert Neisser, M.D.
Medical Director, Neve On Government Hospital (Bnai Brak, Israel). Education: Birmingham University and Hadassah Medical School of the University of Jerusalem.

Philip G. Ney, M.D., M.A., FRCP(C).
Psychiatrist (Victoria). Education: University of British Columbia, McGill University, University of London, University of Illinois, Faculty Appointments: University of British Columbia. Publications: Author of numerous articles.

Myre Sim, M.D., Ch.B., FRCP(C).
Professor of Psychiatry, University of Ottawa Faculty of Medicine. Education: Edinburgh University. Faculty Appointments: Birmingham University. Publications: Author of numerous books and articles.

Jolie Siebold Zimmer, M.A.
Director, Pregnancy Aftermath Helpline, Inc. (Milwaukee). Education: Mount Mary College, University of North Carolina. Faculty Appointments: Holy Redeemer College.

Index